D1105096

This special printing
has been limited to
one hundred copies.

This copy is presented to

The Honorable Walter R. Peterson

on behalf of

The Thayer School of Engineering

and

Dartmouth College

by

David V. Ragone

THE FIRST HUNDRED YEARS OF THE THAYER SCHOOL

"A centennial is a time to look ahead—not blindly but from the perspective of the past."

The First Hundred Years of The Thayer School of Engineering at Dartmouth College

BY

William Phelps Kimball

WITH A FOREWORD BY

DEAN DAVID VINCENT RAGONE

AND CHAPTERS BY

Professor Edward Stickney Brown

Professor Joseph John Ermenc and

Professor Alvin Omar Converse

The University Press of New England

Hanover · New Hampshire

Library of Congress Catalogue Card Number 70–166977
International Standard Book Number 0–87451–056–2

Printed in the United States of America by
The Stinehour Press, Lunenburg, Vermont

Contents

APPENDIXES

Photographs may be found following page 68. Except as noted, all photographs are from Dartmouth College and Thayer School Archives.

Foreword

AMONG the pleasant surprises that I found since I began my tenure as dean in September 1970 are two that bear directly on the centennial year of the Thayer School. First, I found that an ad hoc committee of the faculty had been formed to plan the celebration of the centennial. Second, I found that the story of the First Hundred Years of the Thayer School was being prepared by former Dean William Kimball. I have been happy to encourage both pursuits.

The centennial year of the Thayer School, or of any organization, is an important one for it provides an opportunity to reexamine the principles and goals of the organization. These opportunities are rare. The "marvels" of modern technology in communication and transportation have, on balance, contributed positively to the quality of life. But, they have created an atmosphere in which it is all too easy to be reached by telephone to answer questions that can wait or to be whisked off around the globe for meetings that may not be necessary. Immediate reaction to external, short-term stimuli is the norm. There is little, if any, time left for reflection and for contemplation.

In an absolute sense, a centennial year has not much meaning. There is nothing fundamental about either concept, centennial or year. Both are the results of man-made conventions. The basis of centennial, the number 100, is a product of our counting scheme. The concept of a year, while clearly having a basis in natural phenomena, is still a quantity defined by man. Thus there is no fundamental significance to this one-hundred-year period of time. Despite the artificiality of the concept, there is still enough fascination with the number 100 to cause people to stop and think. As opportunistic as it may seem, I'm happy to use this occasion to reflect on where we have been and where we are going. The centennial year of the Thayer School, beginning with the Centennial Convocation, is dedicated to this inquiry.

This volume, along with its companion, "The Beginnings of the Thayer School of Engineering at Dartmouth College," is vital in the process for it tells us how we began, what we are, and how we got here. From the outset, the Thayer School has emphasized a professional approach to engineering based on a strong background in the sciences and liberal arts. General Thayer and Robert Fletcher put stress not on the amount of knowledge to be imparted to the student but on "a training which prepares him to acquire readily a minute knowledge of any specialty of the profession to which he may subsequently direct his mind." Reading this volume, I have been impressed with the adherence to this principle throughout the hundred-year history of the school. This stress on professional regeneration is perhaps more important today than it was one hundred years ago.

In the rethinking of the objectives and goals of the School, this book has been useful to me, especially because of my short tenure. The people whom we have invited to help us in this process of reevaluation, the speakers at the Convocation, the administration of the College, the faculty, our students, and our alumni will, I am sure, find it equally useful. I am grateful to the author for his important contribution. I also extend my thanks to Professors Brown, Ermenc, and Converse for authoring chapters of the book and to the Thayer School alumni who contributed to it.

DAVID VINCENT RAGONE
Dean of The Thayer School

Preface

A CENTENNIAL is a time to look ahead, not blindly but from the perspective of the past. Earlier publications have been prepared in order to present particular aspects or more limited periods of the story of Thayer School. They have not, consequently, provided the hundred-year perspective which a centennial book needs. In this book, the authors have sought to supply the longer view.

Ideally, each period in the life of the School should be described by an author who lived it all, as has been done for the last four decades. Unhappily, those who could have written, from equal experience, of the earlier years are no longer able to do so. I have therefore tried to piece together the story of those years from the records at Thayer School, the Baker Library Archives, and the reminiscences of helpful alumni.

Chapters 2 and 11 and the appendixes are concerned with the full hundred-year story of matters for which continuity appears more important than chronology. The remainder of the book has been arranged chronologically in order to reflect the interplay, during a given span of years, among the School's educational philosophy and policies, the dean, the faculty, the students, and the curriculum.

Where it has seemed useful, for the sake of the story, to include material which has appeared in print before, it has been shamelessly but gratefully borrowed. In an attempt to relieve the reader of overexposure to my own prose, I have used quotes in what might otherwise seem an excessive amount. Also, I have sought the recollections of Thayer School alumni, most of them even older than I, to give authenticity, especially to chapter 3. And I have found for the foreword and for chapters 8, 9, and 10, authors who are more to be trusted than I, by virtue of having been either less involved or more involved in the events of those times.

My debt to the coauthors is apparent in the chapters they have written. I am indebted to more than twenty alumni, out of school from forty-five to sixty-seven years, who have furnished reminiscences. Especially to be mentioned are Harold Marston Morse '04, Verney Warren Russell '07, Harry Abbott Ward '10, Peter Staub Dow '11, Whitney Haskins Eastman '11, Nelson Luther Doe '13, Samuel Hobbs '13, Edgar Harold Elkins '15, Richard Henry Ellis '17, Edward Hugo Gumbart, Jr. '17, William James Montgomery '20, Victor Collins Smith '20, Allison van Vliet Dunn '22, Lowell Hoyt Holway '23, and Carl Tracy Washburn '26.

Mrs. Carol S. Moffatt, Associate Editor of The University Press of New England, has contributed much readability and consistency to the book by her meticulous and discriminating review of the manuscript.

In putting together the Thayer School story, the author has learned many things. Among them, he has learned why it is that so many books are dedicated to the author's wife—and so has the author's wife.

To all these and to many others whose words or writings have been quoted, the book owes its value and the author his thanks.

WILLIAM P. KIMBALL
Professor of Civil Engineering Emeritus

The Centennial Convocation

IN OBSERVANCE of the hundredth anniversary of the opening of the Thayer School, the opening of Dartmouth College for the 1971–1972 academic year will feature a three-day convocation on THE NEXT ONE HUNDRED YEARS.

The objective of the convocation is to stimulate a searching discussion of the future by engineers, scientists, social scientists, and humanists.

From the points of view expressed by the participants, insights may be gained into the world's social, environmental, and technological needs of the next hundred years. Future challenges and responsibilities facing engineering education may then be identified to assist Dartmouth and Thayer School, as well as others, to design programs which can give engineering graduates the highest potential for growth and service in their world.

Speakers and session chairmen will include, in addition to President Kemeny, Dean Ragone, and former Deans Kimball and Tribus: Isaac Asimov, science fiction author; Daniel Callahan, Director, Institute of Society, Ethics and Life Sciences, Hastings Center; Donald N. Frey, Chairman of the Board, Bell and Howell Corporation; J. Herbert Hollomon, Consultant to the President and the Provost, Massachusetts Institute of Technology; John Raider Platt, Associate Director, Mental Health Research Institute, University of Michigan; Roger R. D. Revelle, Director, Center of Population Studies, Harvard University; Franklin Smallwood, Orvil E. Dryfoos Professor of Public Affairs, Dartmouth College; James H. Wakelin, Jr., Assistant Secretary of Commerce for Science and Technology, U. S. Commerce Department; Anthony J. Wiener, Chairman, Research Management Council, Hudson Institute; Paul N. Ylvisaker, Professor, Woodrow Wilson School of Public and International Affairs, Princeton University.

The published proceedings containing the ideas and convictions generated by the convocation will provide a permanent record of these concepts and conclusions.

Prologue

December 13, 1769

"[WE] GEORGE the THIRD by the grace of GOD of Great Britain France and Ireland KING Defender of the Faith and so forth . . . DO of our special grace certain Knowledge and mere motion by and with the advice of our Council for said Province by these Presents will, ordain, grant and constitute that there be a College erected in our said Province of New Hampshire by the name of DARTMOUTH COLLEGE for the education and instruction of Youth of the Indian Tribes in this Land in reading, writing and all parts of Learning which shall appear necessary and expedient for civilizing and christianizing Children of Pagans as well as in all liberal Arts and Sciences; and also of English Youth and any others. . . ."[1]

Thus was the ground prepared.

"Braintree, Mass., July 4, 1867.

To the Honorable and Reverend Trustees of Dartmouth College

Moved by a regard for my Alma Mater, and by a consideration of the large demands which the unfolding material interests of the country are sure to make upon our educational Institutions, I have a proposition to present which I hope will meet the approval of your honorable body.

I propose to give to the Trustees of Dartmouth College, in the form either of cash or of good securities, as I may elect, the sum of forty thousand dollars, to be held by them in trust, for the purpose of establishing and sustaining, in connection with that Institution, a School or Department of Architecture and Civil Engineering, . . .

Sylvanus Thayer
Colonel in U.S. Corps
of Engineers &
Brig' General in the
U.S. Army"[2]

And thus was the foundation laid.

1. Dartmouth College Charter.

2. Instrument of Gift No. 1.

CHAPTER 1

Sylvanus Thayer Founds a School

SYLVANUS THAYER—graduate of Dartmouth College and the United States Military Academy, educator, military officer, engineer. Sylvanus Thayer—Father of the Military Academy, elected to the Hall of Fame—and founder of the Thayer School of Civil Engineering. His student days at Dartmouth, his determination to enter military life, his reverence for Napoleon, his lifelong career in the Corps of Engineers, and his seventeen-year service as Superintendent of the Military Academy all conspired to give Dartmouth a school of engineering.

Although Sylvanus Thayer decided on a military career early in life, there was no place for him in the new Military Academy at West Point when he was ready to enter college. Never one to sit and wait, he enrolled at Dartmouth in the fall of 1803 at the age of eighteen, still intent, however, on eventually becoming a cadet at the Military Academy. He stood high in his class—second as a sophomore—and had been elected to Phi Beta Kappa. He had also been chosen to give the valedictory address at the graduation exercises of his class. But three months before his graduation date he left Dartmouth on orders to report to West Point to become a cadet.

The Military Academy which awaited Thayer's arrival in 1807 was barely five years old and had been described by its first Superintendent, Colonel Jonathan Williams, as "like a foundling, barely existing among the mountains." It was a sorry institution. There were no physical or mental requirements for entrance. Class attendance was not required. Even continued residence on the "Hudson Highlands" was not enforced. Discipline was a word unknown in the school's vocabulary. No one knew how many were actually enrolled in the cadet corps but it was far fewer than the 150 authorized by Congress. It was not only a "foundling" but a ne'er-do-well one at that. Little did any one know in March 1807 that the eager cadet who had just arrived from the New Hampshire hills was destined to change all that and to become the "Father of the Military Academy."

Graduated less than a year later as the most brilliant boy in his class, he served one year in the field before being recalled to a one-year term as instructor in mathematics. He was an officer of engineers in the War of 1812 and shortly thereafter he succeeded in winning a two-year assignment in Europe to examine the French and Netherland fortifications, to purchase books for a library at West Point, and to study military schools in France.

When Major Thayer was ordered, at the age of thirty-two, to take over the command of the Military Academy, he found it "in a chaotic condition, without system or regularity in its administration. . . . [He] found himself virtually without a command, the cadets of the Military Academy being mysteriously dispersed to all parts of the country on furlough." After Thayer's arrival, however, "The change from darkness to sunlight at West Point was magical. The academy, which had nodded through several years of comparative stagnation, was suddenly metamorphosed from a drowsy school of supine students to the precocious nonage of a great seminary of science and military art."[1] Cullum may have understated the time required for Thayer to bring about the transformation, but the record is clear that during his sixteen years as Superintendent he did indeed establish the Academy as a school of highest distinction among the military schools of the world.

After leaving West Point in 1833, Thayer served continuously with the Corps of Engineers, of which he became Chief, until his retirement in 1863. During those years, his principal responsibility was the design and construction of the permanent defenses of Boston Harbor.

During his lifetime, Thayer had been a man of remarkable qualities. His contemporaries described him in superlatives: "of heroic mold and stately dignity . . . a scientific soldier and erudite scholar

1. From the address of General George W. Cullum at the unveiling of the statue of General Thayer as "The Father of the Military Academy" at West Point, June 11, 1883.

. . . uniform and just in discipline . . . administering authority with enlightened wisdom . . . a man of outstanding ability and forceful character . . . always spoken of affectionately by the members of the Academic Board and the officers of his staff, and the cadets trained under his firm discipline. . . . [He] won the high regard and admiration of all who served under him." He was certainly a strict disciplinarian, of himself as well as of his subordinates, but he was no martinet, and Robert Fletcher, to whom he entrusted the direction of the School he founded, observed in him "a certain geniality of disposition which possibly was not apparent to many with whom he came in contact."

This was the man who, at the age of eighty-two, found the energy and the wisdom and the perseverance to create, endow, and direct the opening of the Thayer School of Civil Engineering at Dartmouth College. On April 4, 1867, he initiated an exchange of letters with Dartmouth President Asa Dodge Smith which would extend over a period of more than four years leading up to the actual opening of the School in September 1871.

In the meantime, however, Thayer had survived illness, physical injury, frustrations, and disappointments which would have made a man of less persistence and determination give up the fight many times. Glimpses of the events of those four years are furnished by the hundreds of letters which passed between Thayer and President Smith, West Point's Professor Dennis Mahan,[2] and, finally, Thayer Professor of Civil Engineering Robert Fletcher. All of Thayer's letters were written in his own firm, orderly longhand. Many of them, telling the story of the beginnings of the Thayer School, have already been published.[3] It will serve the purpose of this book, therefore, simply to record the major accomplishments.

The first task begun, and one of the last to be finished, was the selection of "a suitable person to fill the Chair" of Thayer Professor of Civil Engineering. For guidance, Thayer turned first to Professor Mahan who suggested Peter S. Michie, a Military Academy grad-

2. A protégé of Thayer's whom he had selected as a cadet some forty-five years earlier to be an instructor at the Military Academy. Mahan, at this time, had been senior Professor of Engineering at the Academy for thirty-five years.

3. Edward Connery Lathem, *The Beginnings of the Thayer School of Civil Engineering at Dartmouth College* (Hanover, N.H.: The Thayer School of Engineering, 1964).

uate of the class of 1863 who was a member of his own staff. Michie promptly declined the proffered chair, preferring the military service. In 1871, however, he was to become a member of the Thayer School Board of Overseers.

Shortly thereafter, President Smith wrote to Thayer, "I have a slight misgiving as to the matter of *salary*. We may find it difficult to secure a man for the moderate sum—$1500—given to our Professors. . . . We may have to give more." Mahan expressed similar misgivings a year later in a letter to the General, saying, "the one great difficulty is the salary. The expense of living has become so great, that men are not willing to relinquish their army commissions for the prospect held out to them in this case."

In the meanwhile, Thayer had assured President Smith that "You need have no 'misgivings' as to the 'salary'. If the right [man] be found & he willing to accept we must have him." We do not know when it was decided to offer the much higher sum of $2,500, but that was the salary rate at which Fletcher was appointed in 1871.

On his return from a visit to West Point where he had met Colonel Michie, President Smith sounded another discouraging note in writing to Thayer: "Indeed there is apt to be a difficulty with men accustomed to military habitudes, about so quiet a place as that we contemplate. If we could find a man who, like yourself, had laid his foundation in College, & had added to it the other necessary Culture, there would be an advantage in it. Ah, I think vainly, as I write, is there no fountain of youth? If *you*, in the fulness of your strength, could take charge of the new Department, how would all our solicitudes vanish."

Smith's statement of job qualifications, however, did not reflect any willingness to compromise. "The qualifications we want," he wrote, "are, 1. A good moral tone, 2. Common Sense, 3. Good original ability, 4. An interest in the proposed line of study, 5. Good attainments in it, 6. A disposition to increase them, 7. Organizing power, 8. Aptness to teach, 9. A gentlemanly bearing." Fortunately for the future of the School, the founder was no more willing to compromise than the President.

During the first three years of the search, no fewer than a dozen men were considered for appointment as Thayer Professor of Civil Engineering. These included, in addition to Michie, General

George L. Andrews USMA '51 (who was to become one of the original members of the Thayer School Board of Overseers), Lieutenant Henry M. Adams USMA '66, Captain Edward C. Boynton USMA '46, Colonel Charles C. Parsons USMA '61, Lieutenant Thomas Tuttle USMA '67, Lieutenant Charles E. L. B. Davis USMA '68, Major William J. L. Nicodemus USMA '58, Mahan's own son Lieutenant Frederic Mahan USMA '67, and Cornell Professor of Civil Engineering William C. Cleveland. Some were found wanting but more declined to accept.

It must have been a great satisfaction, therefore, to Professor Mahan and to the President and to the General when, in June 1870, a man was found who did not hold back and did not procrastinate but immediately responded "that not only would such a career suit him, but that, in coming on duty here [he had been appointed Assistant Professor of Mathematics at the Military Academy the previous year] he had looked forward to qualifying himself for some such place." The man, of course, was Lieutenant Robert Fletcher USMA '68.

Understandably, Thayer and Smith did not procrastinate either. Within two weeks, Fletcher had visited President Smith in Hanover and General Thayer at his home in Braintree, Massachusetts. Fletcher's diary entry for July 9, 1870, referring to the latter visit, notes that "he wishes me to take charge of [the School] until it shall appear whether or not I am competent to go on with it and assume permanent control."

Thus were the long, strenuous efforts of the searchers rewarded by the discovery of the man who was, more than any other individual, to determine the course of the Thayer School for the next half century and to cement an educational philosophy which was to guide the School for at least its first hundred years.

The appraisals which Smith and Thayer exchanged regarding their young professor, however, failed to show unlimited appreciation of his full worth. Wrote Smith, "He is young—but if that be a fault, time will surely correct it. His presence is not very imposing—but as good Dr. Watts said, 'The mind's the standard of the man.' I think there will be no intellectual deficiency. His manners, besides, though simple & unassuming, are easy and gentlemanly. . . . It weighs a little with me that he is of good stock. Judge Richard

Fletcher was his great uncle. . . . [A member of the Dartmouth Class of 1806, Judge Fletcher had left the College a major bequest a year before.] On the whole, if you are satisfied, I think it would be well to appoint him." After interviewing Fletcher and, as we have seen, making him a rather tentative trial offer, Thayer replied, with restrained enthusiasm, "We must take him for better or for worse, at least so as to give him a fair trial; right glad shall I be if he prove to be the right man."

It is, perhaps, not strange that both the President and the General should have some misgivings about offering a professorship to a twenty-three-year-old Army lieutenant at a salary one thousand dollars in excess of the average Dartmouth professor's reward at that time. One hundred years later, one cannot refrain from remarking the parallel of the appointment in 1953 of a twenty-six-year-old Professor of Mathematics who was to become Dartmouth's thirteenth President.

Although the appointment of Fletcher and his acceptance appeared to be an accomplished fact on June 9, 1870, there remained several months of negotiations aimed at securing a leave of absence for Lieutenant Fletcher in order that he not be required to burn his bridges and in order, also, that Dartmouth not be too firmly committed to the untried young professor. So frustrating were the negotiations that at one point the Reverend Dr. Smith was moved to write to General Thayer in military terms, "If the fort is impregnable, it may be a question whether it is best to waste powder and ball upon it." Nevertheless, the lieutenant continued to storm the fort all the way to the White House where President Grant gave him a card for the Adjutant General bearing the message, "There is no objection to giving Lieut. Fletcher a leave of absence for six months to accept a professorship." (signed) "U. S. Grant." However, when Fletcher presented this card to Secretary of War Belknap, the Secretary said that President Grant probably did not understand the matter and that he would talk it over with him and telegraph a final decision. The decision was no and thereupon Lieutenant Fletcher promptly resigned his commission. The Army's loss was Dartmouth's gain. Within the month, Fletcher could inform General Thayer, from Hanover, "I have made a beginning of business here." Thayer School had a professor.

Three and a half years had passed since Sylvanus Thayer's Instrument of Gift had been sent to the Trustees. The search for the professor was the most difficult and demanding task during that period but by no means the only one. Even before the Instrument of Gift was completed, General Thayer, probably mindful of the usefulness of the Military Academy's Board of Visitors which he had initiated, suggested to President Smith that the School should be under the management and control of a Board of Overseers consisting of the President of Dartmouth College and four members taken outside the college. Thayer was anxious to have the Board elected as soon as possible in order to be available to carry on the affairs of the School in the event that his own time might run out before the professor could be appointed and the school established as a going concern.

He and Smith agreed in May 1867 on the people who should be invited to serve with President Smith: Professor Mahan (of course); Professor Oliver P. Hubbard of New Haven, an 1828 graduate of Yale and former member of the Dartmouth faculty who still held an appointment as Lecturer on Mineralogy, Geology, Chemistry, and Pharmacy; General George L. Andrews USMA '51, then U. S. Marshal for Massachusetts and later Professor of French at West Point; and General John C. Palfrey, Harvard '53 and USMA '57, Agent of the Merrimack Manufacturing Company and later Treasurer of the Manchester Mills. They were formally appointed on November 29, 1867, and all, in the words of President Smith, "cheerfully accepted their office." Under date of December 7, 1867, Thayer formally authorized the Board to act for him "in the case of . . . disability on my part." The appointment of overseers had been as supremely simple as the appointment of a professor had been difficult.

Thayer's original Instrument of Gift had proposed to establish and sustain a School of *Architecture and Civil Engineering* and the announcement in the Dartmouth catalogs for both 1868 and 1869 referred to the School in those dual terms. However, in 1869, President Smith suggested to Thayer that the word *Architecture* be dropped from the name of the School, saying, in part, "You will recollect that I spoke to you of a misapprehension which has been somewhat current, in regard to the meaning of the term 'Architecture' in the designation of the Thayer School. It is often understood as meaning Architecture in a broad sense, or as a fine art. This, I know, is not your meaning, but only Architecture as connected with Engineering. . . ." Thayer immediately responded, "I adopt your view as to the title of the school. So let it be called the 'Thayer School of Civil Engineering.' " And so it was called for seventy-two years until, in 1941, the overseers and trustees voted to drop the word *Civil* which by that time had acquired a more limited meaning than had been in the founder's mind.

The reader would be justified in expecting to find in this story of the Thayer School some unambiguous and comprehensive statements by General Thayer himself concerning his philosophy of engineering education and his reasons for selecting Dartmouth to carry out his purposes. Unfortunately, no such statements have been found. Direct sources are limited to intentions ascribed to him at the time by Professor Mahan; to records kept by Professor Fletcher of his many visits with Thayer at his home in Braintree, Massachusetts; to his Programme A, specifying admission requirements; and to correspondence pertaining to Programme A. Such meager information as these sources provide will be presented here. Beyond that, we must reconstruct the General's philosophy of civil engineering education from catalog statements published prior to Fletcher's appointment, from the contents of the first curriculum, and from views ascribed to him by Fletcher shortly after Thayer's death. This reconstruction is at some variance with views ascribed to him fifty and more years later by various writers who had not known him and even with some views expressed by Emeritus Professor Fletcher fifty or sixty years after the fact. Nevertheless, the circumstantial reconstruction is believed to be more reliable than the direct evidence.

Professor Mahan gave an intimation of the General's concept of what the School's program should be when he wrote to President Smith, in connection with the search for the professor, "Such a course of instruction as General Thayer contemplates requires a man of very superior scientific abilities and attainments, to carry it out, and would be a laborious task for the best minds. It contains in fact what is usually distributed among three of four professors in the Continental schools."

In his first report to the Board of Overseers, dated January 22, 1873, Professor Fletcher wrote, "During a year and a half I had a number of interviews with General Thayer and became well acquainted with his plans and expectations for the Thayer School. The more important of these are embodied in numerous memoranda made by me after these interviews, and reviewed by him."[4] Both the memoranda thus referred to and the entries in Fletcher's personal journal are regrettably and surprisingly fragmentary and unrevealing.

His journal entry for July 9, 1871, the first day he spent with Thayer, is rather a long one, but,pertaining to our present interest, notes only, "Had much talk on educational systems in general and the benefits of an 'elective-study' system for our colleges in particular." Only that.

During a visit to Thayer which extended over several days in the spring of 1871, Fletcher made an unusually lengthy entry in his journal based in part on the fact that he "had many interesting conversations with the Gen." But even that entry sheds no light on the General's thoughts about civil engineering education.

Memorandum No. 2 contains some thirty pages of longhand notes dealing with a wide range of topics such as library and books, models, instruments, drawings, the Thayer Mathematical Prize, suggestions for the treasurer, conduct of examinations, form of records, fees, and the arrangement and organization of classes and courses for both the preparatory and the curriculum departments. The only reference to the substance of Programmes A and B are shown in all their essentials in the accompanying facsimile of two pages from Memorandum No. 2 (see pp. 10 and 11). Ambitious but, again, not revealing.

More informative is the following excerpt from Fletcher's first report to the overseers, dated January 22, 1873:

> Gen. Thayer intended the Thayer School to attain, in a few years, the very first position as an Institution for the training of engineers. Basing his plans upon the perfected systems of the European schools, with which he was familiar, especially upon that of l'École des Ponts et Chaussées, probably the first engineering school in the world, he designed that the Thayer School, by confining its course of instruction

4. "Memorandum No. 2. Instructions given to Prof. Fletcher by Gen. Thayer."

Programmes "A" and "B"

Programme "A" to consist of a minute detail ~~synopsis~~ of each of the subjects mentioned among the requisites for admission to the "School." It indicates the minimum of requirements. The requisites shall never be diminished but they may be increased, if deemed proper by the Overseers. It is intended that any young man of intelligence, even if he has to study without instructor, may find in Programme "A", a clear, brief and comprehensive statement of each and every principle and proposition that he is expected to know and demonstrate in each branch.

Programme "B" to include, under general heads, all

subjects which shall be taught in the curriculum. The details and branches may be increased, diminished, modified and arranged as experience shall suggest to the Overseers. But the programme shall never include *more general heads* than at the time of approval by Gen. Thayer. (par. 2, Instrument of Gift, July 4th 1867). These general heads will embrace or include every *branch* which it is possible and proper for a course of the proposed scope to take in, so as to afford as much knowledge as possible on every subject essential and useful to a civil engineer. At the same time a proportion of time must be appropriated to each subject according to its relative im-

entirely to branches of Civil Engineering and to auxiliary subjects, and by requiring the highest standard of attainment, should train only men having a high order of scientific ability, to become ornaments to the profession.

It had been General Thayer's intention to prescribe in full detail both the entrance requirements and the curriculum, identified in his Instrument of Gift as Programmes A and B. But the task grew to proportions far beyond his expectations and proved to be too much even for his remarkable energy and ability. The records are clear, however, that Programme A reached a rather advanced stage under his personal surveillance before his death in September 1872. In fact, it was completed only a few months later. Fletcher's journal entry for April 30, 1873, noted, " 'Programme A' printed, bound and distributed as far as necessary. This long task finally off my hands."

Much of the correspondence between Thayer and Smith and between Thayer and Fletcher pertaining to admission requirements, and therefore indirectly to curriculum, is included in "The Beginnings of the Thayer School." There is abundant evidence that Thayer set very high standards for his School and that most educational institutions fell short of the standards which he believed they should have had. For example, in November 1870, President Smith wrote to Thayer, "It became apparent, some time since, that your requisites for admission to the 'Thayer School' were, in some points, beyond the Curriculum, not only of Dartmouth College, but of any other College in New England." Such views, however, only confirmed Thayer's estimate of the weakness of college curricula and in no way persuaded him to lessen the requisites for admission to *his* School. Again, Professor Fletcher's first report to the Board of Overseers stated that "the standard for admission was to be very high, and the course of instruction was to be ultimately a very advanced one in all its details."

In transmitting his first Instrument of Gift, Thayer had predicted that Programme A, "which is near completion, will fill ten sheets of letter paper." As finally completed and published, it combined the efforts of Thayer, Mahan, Fletcher, Professors Church and Michie of the Military Academy, Professor Peck of Columbia, and Charles A. Young, Appleton Professor of Natural Philosophy and Professor of Astronomy at Dartmouth. Instead of ten sheets of letter paper it filled 196 printed pages. The 118 pages devoted to mathematics, the 70 pages devoted to physics, and the 7 pages on physical geography will not be reproduced here. However, it is possible to show the contents of the page which describes the non-technical requisites.

ENGLISH GRAMMAR.

The applicant must be well versed in the principles of the orthography, etymology, and syntax of the language, and must be able to analyze and parse any sentence.

GEOGRAPHY.

Required, a knowledge of the grand divisions of the earth and all their important political and other sub-divisions, as to their boundaries, dimensions and principal geographical features; relative strength and resources of the leading nationalities and peoples,—their commerce, productions, chief cities, towns, etc. A particular knowledge of the geography of the United States.

HISTORY.

An acquaintance with all the important events of American History, from the discovery of the continent to the present time, is required.

A fair knowledge of the *Outlines of General History* is an important element in any course of education. The student is advised to give some time to the subject, during the Preparatory Course.

Another glimpse of Thayer's philosophy appeared in the Dartmouth College catalog for 1867–1868, as shown in the following:

THAYER SCHOOL OF ARCHITECTURE AND CIVIL ENGINEERING.

By a donation of $40,000 tendered to the Trustees, and accepted by them at their last meeting, Gen. Sylvanus Thayer, of Braintree, Mass., has made provision for establishing, in connection with the College, a special course of instruction in Architecture and Civil Engineering. This munificence had its origin not merely in a regard, on the part of the venerable donor, for his Alma Mater, but in a foresight of the large demand for high attainments in this particular line, which the unfolding material resources of our Country are sure to make; and in a conviction that an increasing number of our young men are disposed to select it as their profession. The Department is to be essentially, though not formally, post-graduate. The requisites for admission will, in some leading branches—particularly in Mathematics—embrace not less, and probably more, than the usual College curriculum. The course of study is to be of the highest order, passing beyond what is possible in Institutions for general culture, and is designed to prepare the capable and faithful student for the most responsible positions and the most difficult service. It will extend through at least two years, each divided into a Winter and Summer Term, and a portion of the latter being given to out-door practice. Temporary employment in Civil Engineering will occasionally be permitted, such as will conduce to the student's improvement, while it will be more or less remunerative. In the arrangement of details, reference will be had to the best methods, both in this country and in Europe. A suitable diploma will be given, on satisfactory examination, to those who complete the course.

It will not be practicable to complete the necessary preparation for opening the school to students, before another College Year. Due notice will be given of the time of opening, the requisites for admission, the course of study, and other particulars.

The words "essentially, though not formally, postgraduate" appeared here for the first time. What did Thayer and Smith have in mind? Certainly not that graduation from college was required, or it would have been so stated. The fact is that fifteen of the first hundred students admitted to Thayer School up to 1894 had had no college education. Whatever General Thayer's philosophy may have been, it apparently did not demand that a civil engineering student should first be a college graduate.

Specific information on admission requirements first appeared in the College catalog for 1870–1871, still prior to Fletcher's influence, where details of the mathematics and physics requirements are shown. The catalog also states that "a Preparatory Class has been formed, which is open to any who wish to complete the requisites for admission, on their passing a satisfactory examination in English Grammar, Physical Geography, Arithmetic, Algebra, Geometry, Plane and Spherical Trigonometry, Mensuration, Surveying and Leveling."

Nor did the curriculum of the School itself provide any opportunity for the student to acquire formal cultural or liberal learning. Therefore, contrary to what has become popular belief, the early records, at least, give no indication that General Thayer considered formal education in the liberating arts essential for the civil engineer.

Some fifty-five years later, Emeritus Professor Fletcher's recollection was at variance with the early records, for in February 1925 he wrote:

> In several interviews with General Thayer during the period from the summer of 1870 to the autumn of 1872, when he died, he stated and restated his purpose in founding the school of civil engineering at Dartmouth College. [Programme A] did not include subjects of general culture, such as English Literature, History, Rhetoric or languages either ancient or modern, because he said that men able to pass the prescribed examination in Mathematics and Physical Science must have had the equivalent of a college training. . . . Consequently it was expected that a college course of four years must precede the two years required for the programme of civil engineering studies.[5]

Nevertheless, the record is clear that the broadening of the admission requirements was gradually accomplished in the years following General Thayer's death.

Turning now to the first curriculum of the School as an expression of General Thayer's philosophy, we find a letter from Professor Mahan to him, dated September 27, 1867, forwarding "General Programmes that I have drawn up. These last comprise, I think, all that you wish to have taught at the school at Dartmouth, and I hope will be found sufficient for any one conversant with the branches of instruction to construct complete detailed programmes from."

Although Programme B was never formally completed, the first curriculum was based solidly on Mahan's general programmes. The subjects of this course of study, "designed to prepare the faithful student for the most responsible positions and the most difficult service," constituted a very complete description of civil engineering in the 1860s. In addition to continuing a few of the admission requisites, the curriculum included the fourteen courses shown herewith.

5. Statement of Professor Fletcher to the Executive Committee of the Thayer Society of Engineers on the Aim and Purpose of the Thayer School.

A complete course in Surveying.
Mechanics of Engineering: applications of the principles of statics, dynamics, mechanics of fluids and mechanics of gases.
Stereotomy.
Cinematics.
Stationary and locomotive steam engines, and the various simple machines, as cranes, pile-engines, etc. used in construction.
Building materials.
Construction of masonry and foundations.
Construction and maintenance of common roads and railroads.
Construction and repair of bridges and roofs.
Construction and maintenance of canals; river, harbor and sea-coast improvements.
Drainage; irrigation; distribution of water.
Practical Astronomy.
Mineralogy and geology.
General principles of architecture; rules applying to the erection of buildings generally.

Mahan had not exaggerated in writing to President Smith that it contained "what is usually distributed among three or four professors in the Continental schools."

Financing his school was the other major task which occupied General Thayer between April 1867 and October 1871. Having decided to contribute or bequeath virtually all of his considerable fortune to education, he had only to designate the proportion for each beneficiary. His residual estate contained the lion's share of some $300,000 for the establishment and endowment of the Thayer Academy at Braintree. Another sizeable amount, about $32,000, went to a building and book fund for the Braintree Library. To Dartmouth College went contributions, during the last four years of his life, amounting to about $70,000, "for the purpose of establishing and sustaining" the Thayer School. An additional amount of $12,000 was conditionally offered to Dartmouth by a codicil of his will.

It is clear that Thayer intended to endow the Thayer School of Civil Engineering richly enough to enable it to be financially independent. His preliminary estimate of the endowment needed was $34,000, but even before tendering his first Instrument of Gift in

July 1867, he had decided to increase his gift to $40,000. Apparently he gradually became aware that more funds would be needed, for by October 1871 he had added gifts bringing the total endowment to approximately $70,000. President Smith had undoubtedly assisted him toward this realization. In fact, in the spring of 1869 in a letter which may not have been entirely ingenuous, he wrote to Thayer, "Perhaps you have learned that Judge Fletcher[6] has left us a residuary bequest, which . . . will amount to $100,000. The income of it is to be used at the discretion of the Trustees.

"For this I feel that we are greatly indebted to you—to your example, if not to your more direct influence. The will is dated Sept. 28, 1867, some time after the announcement of your munificent gift. That gift had doubtless its influence with the Judge. 'So shines a good deed in a naughty world.' Many thanks to you for this new relation of your liberality."

How much travail over how many years would have been spared how many people connected with the Thayer School had the deed shone brightly enough to persuade the trustees to apply the income from Judge Fletcher's bequest to the operation of Director Fletcher's school!

With the School generously endowed, the overseers appointed, and the professor on the job, General Thayer might have rested. But first, with Fletcher's assistance, he made one more enduring gift to the School in the form of a library of nineteenth-century and earlier books, manuscripts, and plates of engineering in Europe and the United States. Even then unwilling to sit back, he gave a guiding hand to the professor in all the affairs of establishing the School as a going concern and conducting it through its first year of life. In September of 1872, one year after the opening of his School and only a few days after his last letter of instructions to Professor Fletcher, Sylvanus Thayer died.

6. As recorded previously, with the appearance two years later of Professor-candidate Robert Fletcher, President Smith had noted with satisfaction that he was a great nephew of Judge Fletcher.

CHAPTER 2

The Overseers Manage a School

General Thayer's Instrument of Gift reposed extraordinary responsibility and authority in the Board of Overseers. The management of the School was vested in it. It was to fix and annually revise the requisites for admission and the course of studies, all, however, "in strict accordance with . . . Programmes [A and B] hereto appended." The Board was to make rules respecting the teachers and students but, in relation to deportment, it was understood that the students were subject to the laws of the College. The overseers were to elect all the teachers, subject to approval by the Trustees of the College, and could remove them by majority vote. They were also to determine the salaries of the professor and the teachers and the rate of tuition. Finally, the income from Thayer School funds, "whether contributed by myself, or added by others," was to be disbursed by the treasurer of the College on order of the president "given in accordance with the directions of the Board of Overseers."

General Thayer's directive to the Board to manage the School was followed quite literally for almost eighty-five years. During the early years, the management activities consisted principally of adoption of admission requirements, approval of curriculum, attendance at examination of degree candidates, recommending the granting of degrees, and budgeting expenses. These activities were continued in varying amount, depending on the year-by-year demands, until the Board's reorganization in 1957. At that time, the trustees reaffirmed and clarified the Board's functions as originally stated and redefined them as being "advisory to the President and Trustees of Dartmouth College with respect to: the program and management of the School; reports of the Dean; and any matter referred to it by the President or Trustees pertaining to the Thayer School or its relationship with the College, including among others, curricular, administrative, and financial matters."

Tenure on the Board was originally for life. The average length of term prior to the 1957 reorganization was nineteen years. General Palfrey's thirty-nine years was the longest term if Professor Fletcher's sixty-three years of service, the first forty-five as the professor meeting with the Board and the last eighteen as Board member and clerk, are discounted. Appendix A contains a list of Board members serving during the School's first hundred years. Concurrence and length of terms may be more readily observed in the two bar graphs contained in this chapter.

Although the Board was appointed in 1867, it took no actions as a Board and did not convene its first meeting until May 20, 1873. In the meantime, much had happened as told in the previous chapter. Also, to the great distress of both Thayer and Fletcher, Overseer Dennis Mahan had died by drowning in September of 1871. He was replaced on the Board by Professor Michie whom he had once approached to accept appointment as the original Thayer Professor.

Professor Fletcher deemed it necessary to submit two lengthy reports to the Board at its first meeting. These reports filled twenty-six pages of carefully composed and meticulously inscribed information on all aspects of the School. So detailed were they that the Board was moved to pass a resolution "that the Professor be recommended to reduce his official writing to the least volume necessary to keep a correct general account of his department." Nevertheless, a precedent had been set. The annual Dean's Report to the Board of Overseers became the means of providing the Board with the information considered necessary for the performance of its duties. Except for three years, 1887 to 1889 when the reports were made only verbally, for the next eighty-four years they were written out in varying detail by Fletcher and his successors, frequently with supporting attachments. The most voluminous, surpassing even Professor Fletcher's 1873 report, were the sixty-page reports of 1954 and 1955.

Attendance at the examination of degree candidates was a duty which members of the Board probably enjoyed more than did the

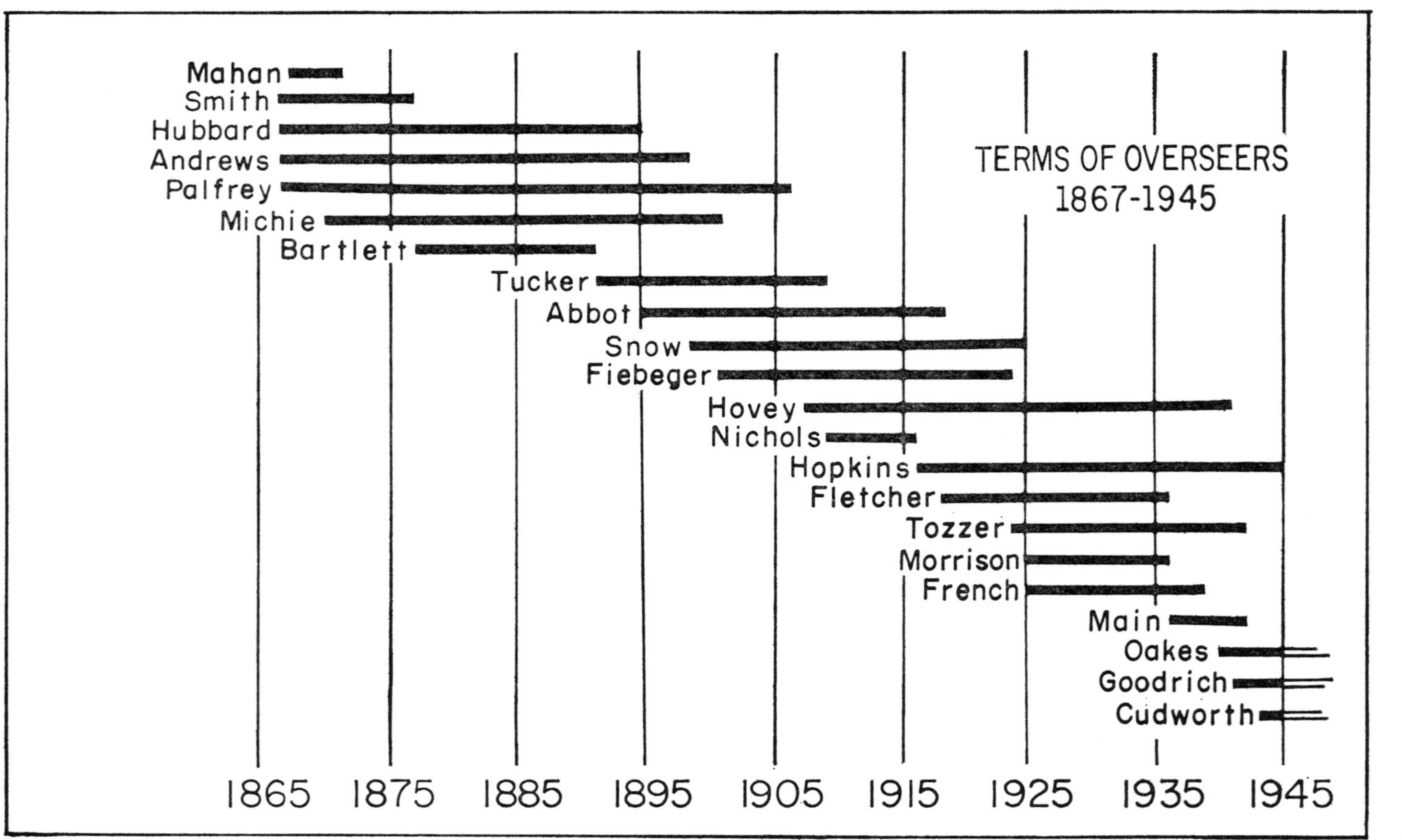

TERMS OF OVERSEERS
1867-1945
Mahan
Smith
Hubbard
Andrews
Palfrey
Michie
Bartlett
Tucker
Abbot
Snow
Fiebeger
Hovey
Nichols
Hopkins
Fletcher
Tozzer
Morrison
French
Main
Oakes
Goodrich
Cudworth
1865
1875
1885
1895
1905
1915
1925
1935
1945

Figure 1

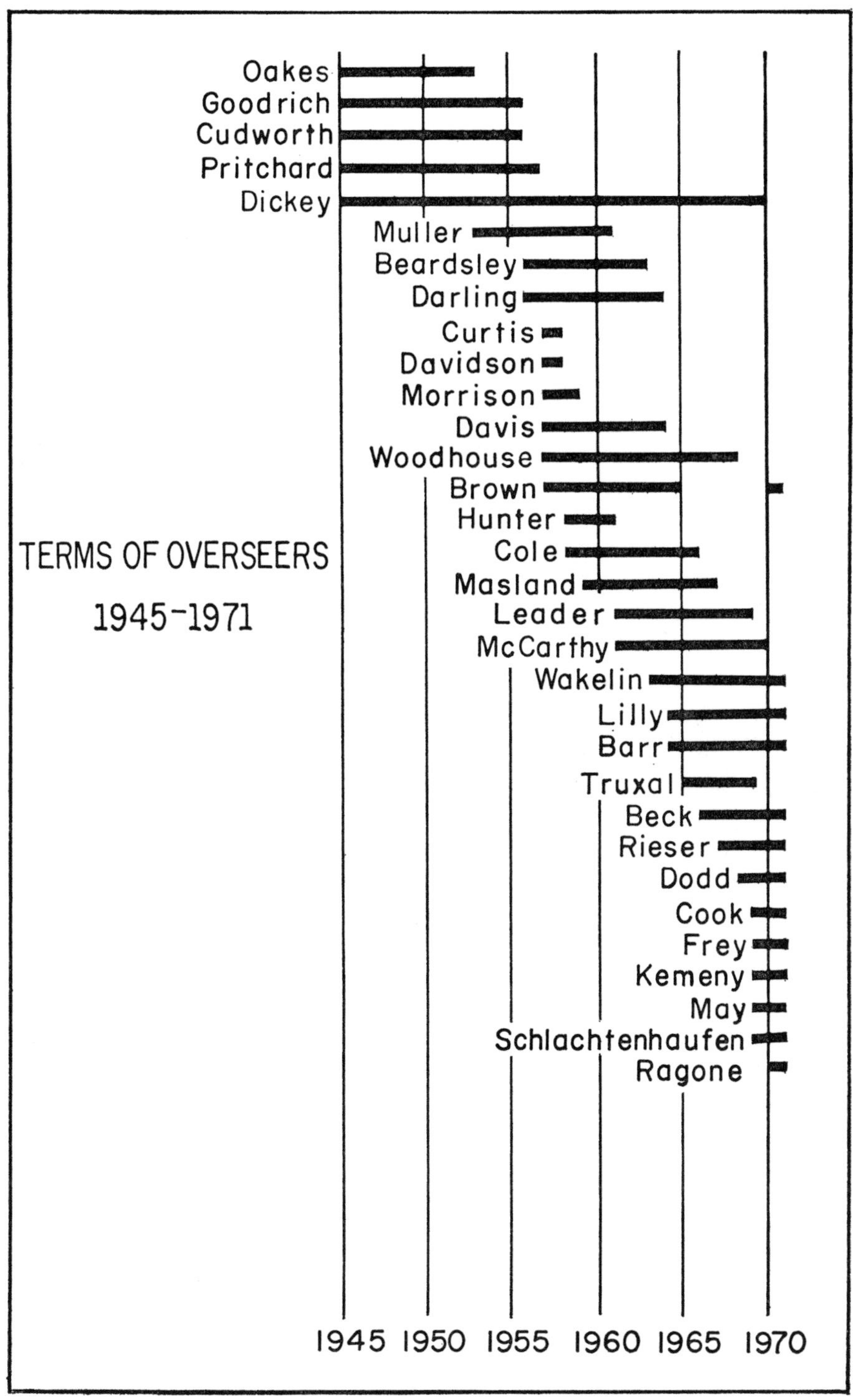
Oakes
Goodrich
Cudworth
Pritchard
Dickey
Muller
Beardsley
Darling
Curtis
Davidson
Morrison
Davis
Woodhouse
Brown
Hunter
Cole
Masland
Leader
McCarthy
Wakelin
Lilly
Barr
Truxal
Beck
Rieser
Dodd
Cook
Frey
Kemeny
May
Schlachtenhaufen
Ragone
TERMS OF OVERSEERS
1945-1971
1945
1950
1955
1960
1965
1970

Figure 2

candidates. It was a duty scrupulously observed during the first twenty years. It took a different form in 1894 when, in lieu of attending examinations, the Board listened to candidates' reports on theses or special projects and examined each candidate individually on his topic. This practice was followed for forty years until, beginning in 1936, candidates were again examined on the full breadth of their studies. A casualty of World War II, the practice has not been resumed.

On recommendation of the Board of Overseers, the Trustees of the College in June 1953 authorized a committee to study the organization of the Board "for the purpose of recommending any changes in the structure and composition of that Board that may appear advisable to meet present and forseeable needs of the School and the College." The committee, under the chairmanship of Justin A. Stanley, then Vice President of the College, submitted a fifty-page report reviewing the history of the Board and the School's relationship with the College and presenting the following conclusions:

1. Thayer School is part of Dartmouth College and subject to the ultimate authority of the Trustees of the College.

2. So long as the Trustees continue to make use of the Thayer funds in the operation of the Thayer School, they must do so on the basic conditions specified by General Thayer.

3. Those conditions are not to be confused with specific details of operation set out in the Instrument of Gift, as amended, but should be taken in their broad sense of a quality engineering course for men who are first trained in the liberal arts.

4. The management of the School, within the general supervision of the Trustees, rests in the Board of Overseers.

5. The Board is self-perpetuating and would seem to have the power to fix the terms of its members.

6. The Board has the right to elect members proffered by the Dartmouth Society of Engineers, though it cannot be compelled to do so by that Society. [The Board has, however, chosen to do so since its adoption of the plan in 1925.]

7. The Board would seem to have the power to expand its membership if in its opinion such expansion is desirable for the best management of the School under changed conditions.

8. In view of the fact that Thayer funds cover so little of the operating costs of the School, it is arguable that the Trustees could expand the Board, naming additional Overseers, whose primary duty would not be with reference to the Thayer funds.

The Stanley committee also recommended that the membership of the Board be increased from five to nine, that it include, whenever possible, at least one Trustee of Dartmouth College, and that members be elected for four-year terms with a maximum of two successive terms. These recommendations were immediately endorsed by the overseers and became effective in 1957 on adoption by the College Trustees in conjunction with broader revisions of the program and organization of the School resulting from the work of the Trustees Planning Committee.

In 1969, it became apparent to the Board that, in the interest of better serving the School's developing program, its membership should be further expanded. This expansion established the membership of the Board to consist of the President and the Provost of Dartmouth College, the Dean of the Thayer School, and twelve elected members of whom six are nominated by the Trustees of Dartmouth College, three by the Dartmouth Society of Engineers and three by the Board itself, the terms of elected members to be three years. The Board was required to meet at least twice a year.

The service rendered to the School by its Board of Overseers over the years has gone far beyond the mechanics of management. In recent years, it has been less concerned with management details and more with overall policy, directing its attention from time to time to the issues which appeared to be most urgent. In this manner, it has continued its invaluable service to the School. The distinguished members have been a continuing inspiration to students and faculty. Their wise counsel on many matters pertaining to philosophy, policy, and program has helped immeasurably to keep up both the morale and the aims of the School through times of crisis as well as times of prosperity.

General Thayer could not have anticipated that his generous gifts would prove totally inadequate to enable the School to achieve his objectives almost from the very beginning. But the $3,500 income from the Thayer Fund could not do a great deal more than meet Professor Fletcher's ample salary. A reproduction of a portion of the minutes of the first overseers meeting, held May 21, 1873, illustrates the point (see p. 24).

The money could not be found to employ another full-time teacher even at practically starvation wages during the first several

3d. That the appropriation of money for the year 1873–4 be as follows:

1. Professor's salary,	$2500.00
2. Instruction,	200.00
3. Books and instruments,	250.00
4. Fuel and expenses of recitation rooms,	50.00
5. Reserve to be disposed of on recommendation of the Board of Overseers, {more or less}	148.80
6. Reserve for the President of the Board of Overseers (incidentals),	250.00
7. Expenses of the Board of Overseers, {more or less}	101.20
	$3500.00

years and it was not until 1883 that a teacher of anything more than minimal qualifications could be appointed. The bar graph on page 25 clearly shows the constraints on faculty which were imposed by the inadequacy of the endowment income.

By the end of his second full year as the one and only director and full-time teacher on the staff, Fletcher began to have misgivings with regard to the feasibility of achieving Thayer's lofty objectives. These misgivings he expressed to the overseers in no uncertain terms. "We find that the institutions named [Rensselaer, MIT, Sheffield School of Yale, Union College, Columbia University] have full corps of able and experienced instructors, ample means, necessary models and instruments and appliances of various kinds. We have very limited means, a single Professor and few models, instruments or other appliances of any kind.

"Gentlemen, the prevailing tone of this report may seem desponding. But I am not despondent. On the contrary, I have great hopes of a bright future for the Thayer School. . . . I have endeavored merely to look at matters and set them forth as they are, not as I wish they were, or hope they may be. Certainly, from personal

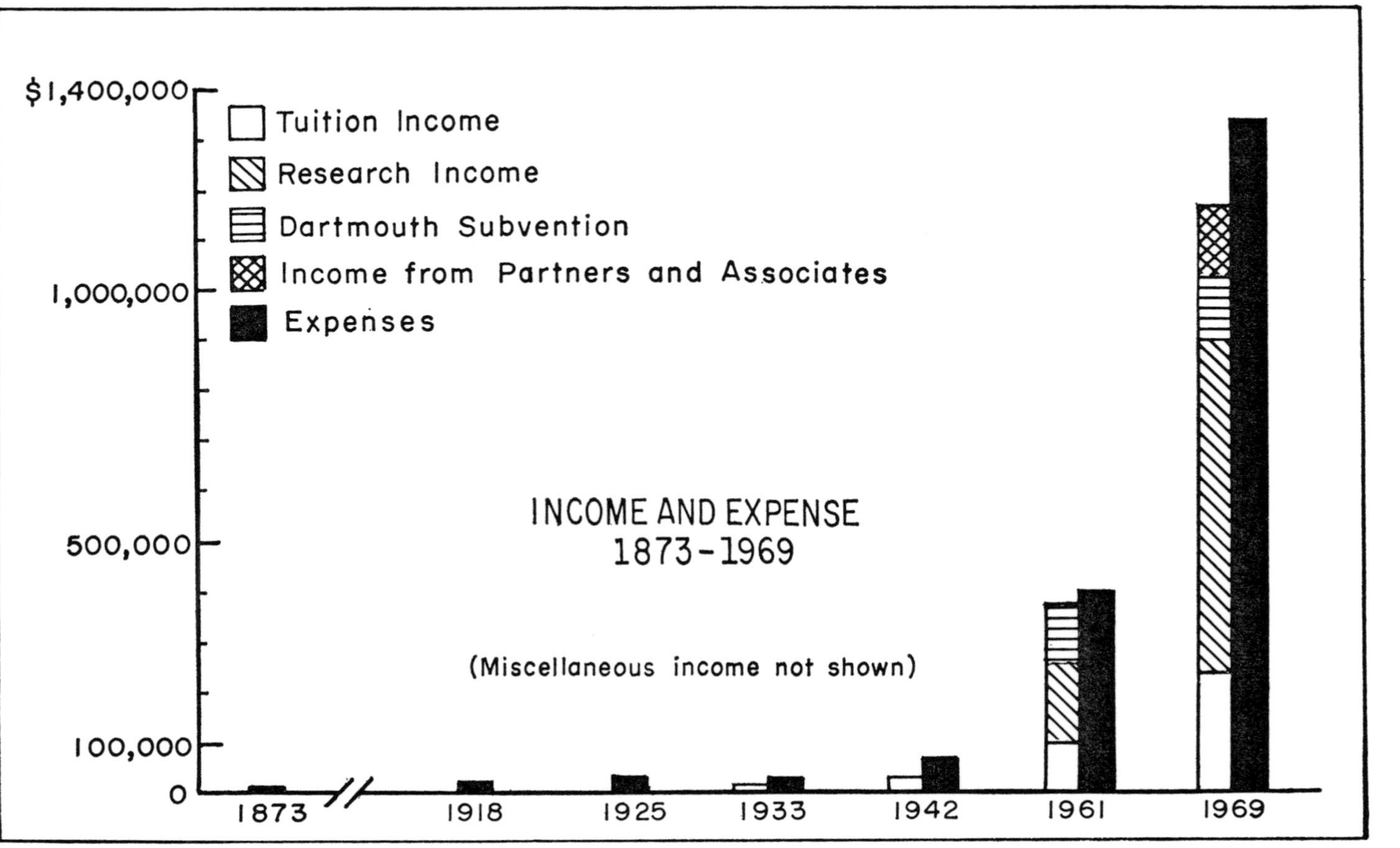
$1,400,000
1,000,000
500,000
100,000
0
Tuition Income
Research Income
Dartmouth Subvention
Income from Partners and Associates
Expenses
INCOME AND EXPENSE
1873-1969
(Miscellaneous income not shown)
1873
1918
1925
1933
1942
1961
1969

Figure 3

considerations, I should try to show off everything to the best possible advantage.

"I am ready and willing to undertake, in the interests of the School, the performance of just so much as I conscientiously feel to be able to accomplish faithfully and well. But I decline to undertake another year, to do the work which should be divided at least among two or three, or, better, among four. . . . To endeavor or pretend to do more than we can faithfully and honestly perform, would be unjust to the Thayer School and its founder, unjust to ourselves, and unjust to those who put themselves under our charge." In spite of this strong plea, the overseers found themselves unable to budget a second full-time instructor until three years later, and then only on a year-to-year basis.

The story of the recurring problem of financing can best be told in the chronological chapters of this book. The present discussion is intended to set the framework and provide the perspective for that story. For this purpose, the accompanying table and the bar graph on page 25 summarize annual expense and income for years generally corresponding to the beginnings and endings of the chronological chapters. The figures for 1872–73 have been taken from Thayer School records; all others have been assembled by the editor from published annual reports of Dartmouth College and present a true comparison of income and expense for the years shown. The year 1941–42 is shown instead of 1944–45 because it is more representative of the longtime trend and because of the way in which financial reports were presented during World War II years. Thayer School was totally engaged in providing instruction for Navy V-12 students enrolled in the College and for Navy Civil Engineer Corps students. However, none of the payments made to the College by the Navy in lieu of tuition were shown in the financial reports as Thayer School credits.

Faculty salaries have always been a major portion of the School's expense, just as tuition payments have been a major portion of its income. The graph on page 28 shows the growth in faculty salaries as reflected in the average salary of the School's full professors and the more or less parallel growth in tuition charge. Tuition charges have generally played a larger part than enrollment in increasing the School's tuition income.

EXPENSE AND INCOME FOR SELECTED YEARS

Year	*Expense*	*Tuition Income*	*Research Income*	*College Contrib.*[1]	*Thayer Society Gift*[2]	*Amos Tuck Fund*[3]	*Other Income Used*[4]
1872–73	3,504	108	0	0	0	0	3,396
1917–18	11,140	2,414	0	0	1,333	2,000	5,393
1924–25	18,743	3,658	0	0	6,750	8,000	335
1932–33	14,715	8,400	0	0	1,000[5]	1,000	3,775
1941–42	29,460	16,703	0	413	3,200[6]	1,000	8,144
1960–61	437,190	96,855	186,527	135,707			18,101
1968–69	1,355,819	256,087	595,781	197,000			306,951[7]

Notes:

1) College contributions began in 1936 and from 1936 to 1969 totaled $2,849,000.

2) Thayer Society of Engineers gifts began in 1905 and from 1905 to 1943 totaled $86,000, including allocations from the Dartmouth Alumni Fund 1938–43.

3) Allocations from the Amos Tuck Endowment for Increase of Salaries were made annually from 1912 to 1942 and totaled $83,000.

4) Other income used to balance expense includes income from endowment funds, gifts, and miscellaneous sources.

5) Approximation.

6) Allocation from Dartmouth College Alumni Fund.

7) Partial breakdown for 1968–69 is shown in the table on page 29.

The table on page 29 shows principal and income of Thayer School endowment funds according to the Dartmouth Financial Report for 1968–69. It should be noted that the Ford Foundation and Sloan Foundation funds are considered expendable. The principal of all other Thayer School endowment funds in 1968–69 amounted to approximately $350,000 of which $150,000 is the amount to which General Thayer's $70,000 gifts of 1867–71 have appreciated.

In summary, from 1871 to 1948 all income to meet current expenses was derived from tuition, endowment income, and gifts for scholarships and general purposes. In 1947–48, the first research income was received as noted later in chapter 9. Grants and contract payments for research were to grow to a major source of income through the 1950s and 1960s. The greatly increased operating expenses during the 1960s were made possible by increased College subventions, large gifts from the Sloan Foundation and the Ford Foundation, and annual payments from Thayer School's Industrial Partners and Associates. More information on these sources will be found in chapter 10.

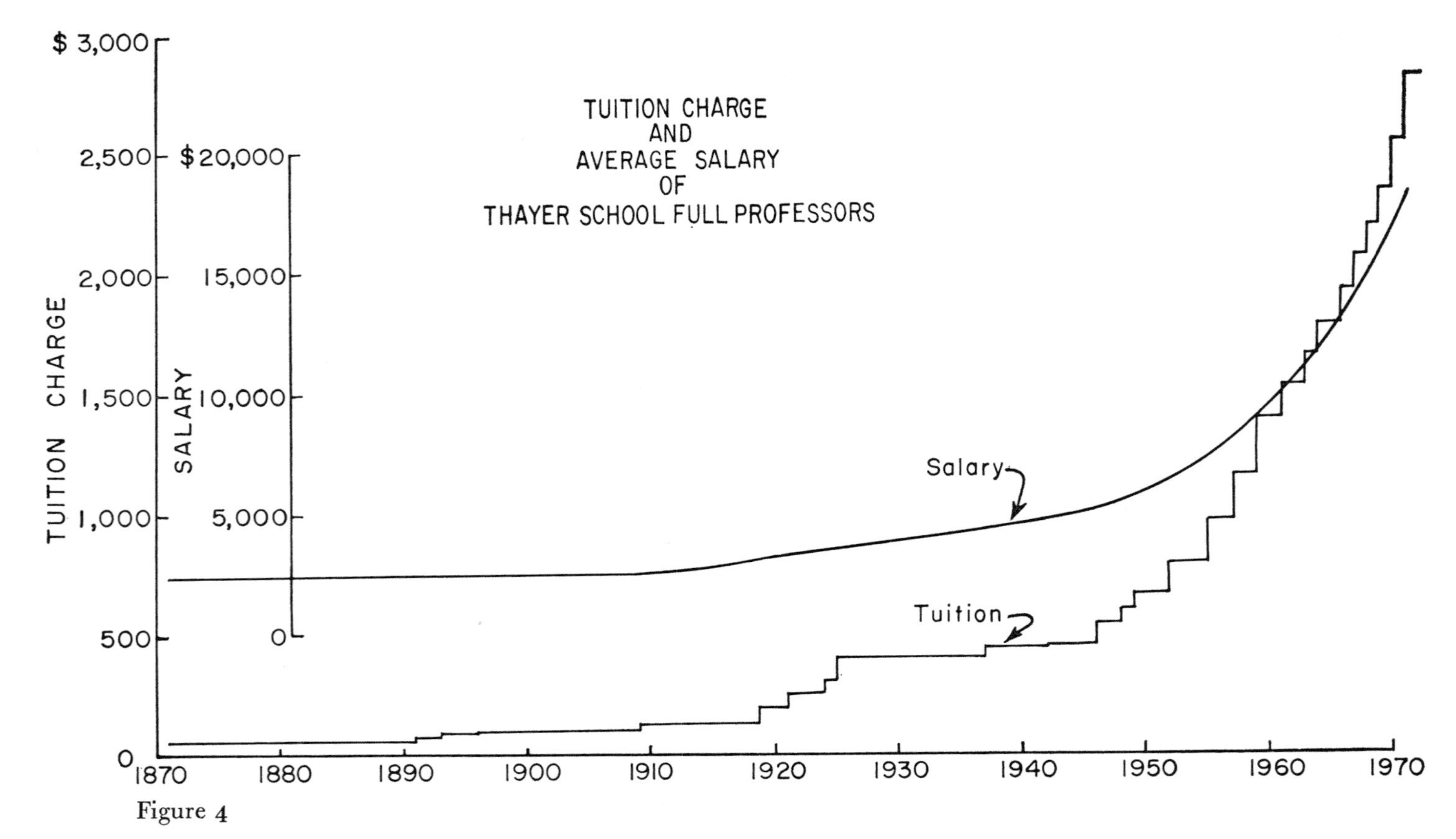
TUITION CHARGE
AND
AVERAGE SALARY
OF
THAYER SCHOOL FULL PROFESSORS
$ 3,000
2,500
2,000
1,500
1,000
500
0
TUITION CHARGE
$20,000
15,000
10,000
5,000
0
SALARY
Salary
Tuition
1870
1880
1890
1900
1910
1920
1930
1940
1950
1960
1970

Figure 4

THAYER SCHOOL ENDOWMENT FUNDS

For Instruction and Other General Purposes	*Principal June 30, 1969*	*Net Income for 1968–1969*
Bryant Chucking Grinder Company	$ 5 000 00	$ 503 68
Common Fund (in part)	230 00	11 24
Frank E. 1901 and Elsie M. Cudworth	2 000 00	183 30
Frank W. Daniels 1878 (⅓ Thayer)	28 869 90	3 132 15
Dartmouth Society of Engineers	7 100 00	775 50
Robert Fletcher 1871 H	5 000 00	154 63
Ray T. Gile 1877 Fund No. 2	915 00	107 15
Jones & Lamson Machine Company	25 000 00	2 515 39
Lovejoy Tool Company	2 000 00	201 23
John S. MacDonald 1914TH Memorial	2 475 00	208 93
Merritt-Chapman & Scott Corporation	1 000 00	65 28
Edwin J. Morrison 1890 Memorial	25 000 00	1 922 16
Richard E. Pritchard 1914	3 180 94	213 48
Arthur W. Stone 1894 Memorial Fund	1 000 00	42 28
Sylvanus Thayer 1807 Fund No. 1 (SIE)	150 351 75	12 012 26
Thomas T. Whittier 1899	5 000 00	253 73
	$264 122 59	$22 302 39
For Scholarships and Other Student Aid		
Arthur W. Chase 1880	5 799 55	691 58
Herbert F. Darling 1926	16 632 00	1 722 03
George W. Davis Memorial	26 157 69	2 837 90
Luther S. Oakes 1899	37 738 48	2 369 41
	$ 86 327 72	$ 7 620 92
For Other Purposes		
The Ford Foundation Fund No. 5—(SIE)	$ 21 459 68	$ 925 00
The Sloan Foundation Fund No. 2—(SIE) (Expendable)	494 597 33	4 886 09
	$516 057 21	$ 5 811 09
Total	$866 507 32	$35 734 40

INCOME FROM GIFTS

	Credited to 1968–1969
Associates Program Reserve	$ 21,000
Partnership Program Reserve	120,000
Other Reserves	6,376
Graduate Support and Instruction	4,040
Scholarships	23,385

The management of the School included, of course, provisions for housing. The story of the School's peregrinations began with the occupation of rooms in the Dartmouth Row buildings in 1871 but the background of the housing problem, based on the assumptions General Thayer made in addressing his first Instrument of Gift to the trustees in 1867, began to build up as soon as Fletcher appeared. In a letter dated January 30, 1871, Thayer had written to Fletcher, "In my conversation with President Smith I received the impression—not to say promise—that all the necessary rooms for the School might and would be furnished by the College—but for which I would not have taken measures to open the School."

In the spring of 1871, responding to a gentle suggestion of President Smith's, Thayer added a codicil to his will offering $12,000 to go toward the erection of a library building for the College. He stipulated that the first floor of the building be set apart for the exclusive use of the Thayer School and that, pending completion of the building, the wants of the school should be met and that "no rent will be paid for rooms in Culver Hall, or elsewhere, *without my consent.*" Actually, the conditions of the codicil not being met and a substitute proposal not being acceptable to the trustees of Thayer's estate, the legacy was finally lost to Dartmouth.

Further light was thrown on the General's understanding of the College's obligation by a later memorial which Professor Fletcher wrote to the trustees.

> In the conferences with President Smith, . . . the question of payment of rent for rooms to be assigned was raised. This was submitted to General Thayer in a conference had with him, on his summons, April 19th. He then made to the Director strong protest against the proposition stating that, by his understanding, the acceptance of the trust carried with it the obligation, on the part of the Trustees of the College, to provide suitable rooms for the use of the School.

The acceptance by the College of the obligation to provide quarters for the Thayer School removed, presumably for all time, that particular burden from its always-strained resources.

During the School's first year, Fletcher had the use of five small rooms located in three of the Dartmouth Row buildings. He had purchased stoves for the drawing room and the recitation room, and to keep the cost of fuel down to $25 (the cost of three and a half cords of wood) for the winter he proposed to use one of the rooms only part of the time in cold weather.

In 1874, the College gave the School, free of rent, the use of the entire suite of rooms on the south side of the first floor of Thornton Hall. Apparently the Reed Hall room assigned in 1871 was retained, but no further mention is made of the Wentworth Hall rooms.

Noting the Thornton and Reed space in his 1875 Annual Report, Fletcher wrote, "Thus our accommodations are ample for a few years at least." However, a few paragraphs—not years—later he recommended acquisition of space in Culver Hall which had been completed four years earlier primarily for the use of the Agricultural College.

> During the past two years, the necessity for what may be termed a "Physical laboratory" has forced itself upon the mind of your professor. . . . There can be no doubt that a limited amount of time can be very profitably devoted to experimental operations. . . . It is also convenient to have a room for rough work where the young men may do little jobs of repairing, etc. . . . and thus save the School items of expense . . . while acquiring for themselves useful manual dexterity and mechanical skill. The basement floor of Culver Hall would afford an excellent place for such a purpose. The executive officer of the Agricultural College gives us to understand that no rent will be charged, in consideration of little favors that have been and may be rendered to that Institution by Thayer students, in making occasional surveys as part of their practice.

The room was fitted up at a total cost of about $100, "more than was estimated because it was deemed better to have a larger room, and necessary to put down a floor."

Finally, in 1892, Thayer School moved into its own building and it has continued to be separately housed ever since. This building was located on Park Street just south of Wheelock and had been the New Hampshire Agricultural Experiment Station. Built in 1888, it became available to the alert Professor Fletcher when it was decided to move the Agriculture School to Durham where it was to thrive and, as the University of New Hampshire, to outgrow its early Hanover neighbor. This four-year-old brick building, providing about 6,000 square feet of floor area, was purchased for $3,000. It was a good buy. Presently known as Thayer Lodge, it still serves as a college-owned apartment house.

Even at such a bargain price however, no College funds were immediately available for its purchase. A portion of the price was therefore temporarily met by Professor Fletcher himself. The remaining $1,800 was donated by "generous friends in New York and Boston," solicited by Fletcher's right-hand man Associate Professor Hiram Hitchcock. Professor Fletcher's report of the Board of Overseers 1892 meeting records that "The Board visited the new building and expressed great satisfaction at the purchase." Nevertheless, the overseers seem to have approved Fletcher's part in the transaction with some hesitance, for it is noted that they "wished Prof. Fletcher to have a writing duly executed setting forth his intent to purchase the building only for the use of the Thayer School." Two years later, the College repaid Professor Fletcher the amount of his loan—though not the gifts of the generous friends—and took title to the building, holding it in trust for the School.

In this spacious new home, accommodations were available to house students serving as building custodians, an arrangement which was to be carried through to the School's next home and to be continued until the final move to Cummings Memorial in 1939. The formal agreement executed in August 1898 between student custodian Albert Galusha '00 and Director Fletcher spelled out the conditions of occupancy and employment in minute detail. For example, the custodian was permitted to have one roommate; the rental value for the eight-month period was set at $84, made up of $16 for lights, $24 for heat, and $44 for rent; further, "The custodian agrees not to allow any intoxicating drink or alcoholic beverage to be brought into, kept, or used in the building at any time; also that neither occupant is to 'board himself' in the building or do, or allow, any cooking therein . . . each room to be swept as often as once per week. . . . The keeping of a dog in the building will not be allowed. . . . SMOKING is not to be allowed *in any part of the building* before supper."

Not, however, anticipated or covered by the agreement was an incident recalled recently by Harold Morse '04: "I also recall the day when Toot Worthen ('04) who roomed on the second floor of the T. S. building with Harold Comstock ('04) thought he could go down the stairs on skis. Unfortunately, at the psychological moment when his skis hit the bottom and he kept on going, Bobby

Fletcher came in the door and received Toot in his midriff. I am unable," concludes Morse, "to describe what ensued."

The building survived this and many other, more expectable, events for twenty years until, in 1912, Thayer School enrollment having increased from seven to thirty-six, the space had become completely inadequate and the School moved into Bissell Hall which was to remain its home for twenty-seven years.

Bissell Hall, located at the southwest corner of Wheelock and College Streets, part of the site now occupied by Hopkins Center, had been built in 1867 at a cost of $22,006.44 and was the College gymnasium until 1911 when the present Alumni Gymnasium was occupied. Extensive alterations were required to adapt it to use as an office-classroom-laboratory facility at a cost approaching very nearly the original cost of the building.

The urgent need for larger quarters was emphasized by Director Fletcher in 1907 in discussing with Otis Hovey '89 the raising of capital funds for the School. He and President Tucker had then considered and rejected the possibility of adapting Bissell Hall. The frugal director of Thayer School expressed his estimate of building needs as well as his opinion of architects in writing to Hovey, "The newly instituted Tuck School has managed to spend $125,000 for its building, as I am informed, which, to my mind, is at least $50,000 too much. . . . Holden is working out a plan for a new building . . . which would probably cost . . . at least 60,000 dollars, even if built by the Engineering Department. The architects would fool away $25,000 more on *architectural features*."

A potential donor wishing to have official word of the somewhat vague relationship between the School and the College, the trustees voted on June 22, 1908, that "It is the sense of the Trustees that the Thayer School of Civil Engineering constitutes in fact and substance a post graduate course or department of the College."

However, two years later, a new Dartmouth president having been installed, the memory of the trustees appears to have been less than perfect, judging by their vote on June 20, 1910, "to assign Bissell Hall . . . to the use of the Thayer School . . . and [request] the President . . . to communicate with the owners of the School, advising them that the Trustees do not feel justified at present in undertaking to provide the funds necessary to equip the building for the uses of the School." This wording prompted Overseer Hovey to write to Professor Fletcher, "There is still a misapprehension on the part of the Trustees as to the *ownership of the School*, which misapprehension it will be our duty to remove."

Removing the misapprehension, however, proved to be beyond the overseers' powers of persuasion, and they therefore requested the trustees to grant a loan "to be repaid whenever a sufficient building fund is raised for the Thayer School, by subscription or donation." While it is true that precedents had been established requiring the School to stand the cost of building maintenance and repairs, it seems odd that, in view of the fact that Bissell Hall was wholly unsuited for Thayer School use without the alterations, the overseers were content to request a loan rather than an outright grant.

The trustees thereupon, in October of that year, authorized a loan of $15,000 (later increased to $20,000) to cover the cost of repairs and alterations "upon the definite understanding that the loan shall be repaid from funds to be raised by the Overseers and Friends of Thayer School at the earliest time practicable."

The loan was halved in 1912 by the generosity of Edward Tuck, whose earlier gifts to the College had established the Amos Tuck School of Administration and Finance, and who now directed that $10,000 from the Surplus Income and Reserve account of his fund be used toward the payment of Thayer School's debt to the College for Bissell Hall alterations.

The next move came in 1939 when the College provided Thayer School not only with a home that was all its own but, for the first time, one that was brand new and that was built specifically for the School. This was made possible by a legacy from Jeannette I. Cummings providing for a memorial to her late husband Horace S. Cummings of the Dartmouth Class of 1862. The bequest proved to be sufficient not only to build the original Horace S. Cummings Memorial building in 1939 but also to provide funds toward the cost of expansion in 1947.

In suggesting the move from Bissell Hall, President Hopkins was prompted by a desire to have areas of the campus "functionalized with the undergraduate college as the hub of the whole institution." He undoubtedly also had it in mind that the appearance of the hub could be considerably improved by removing the 1867 gymnasium building.

The Tuck School having created a graduate school center at the west end of Tuck Mall, and President Hopkins desiring to encourage a closer relationship between Tuck and Thayer, that area was selected. He also had in mind the advantages to both schools in sharing the already-available Tuck School dormitories and dining hall.

Although the new building was only about one-third larger than Bissell Hall, careful planning resulted in a feeling of spaciousness which had been quite lacking in Bissell. Actually, Dean Garran had estimated that a considerably smaller, well-planned building would adequately serve the civil engineering curriculum with an enrollment of forty students, seemingly an optimistic goal since the 1937 enrollment was only twenty-four. Fortunately, however, College Architect Larsen designed a building nearly twice the size suggested by the dean.

The Cummings Memorial cornerstone, laid on November 21, 1938, enclosed a sealed box containing the *Dartmouth Alumni Magazine* for that month, the 1937 Thayer School Register, the 1938 Thayer School catalog, the *Dartmouth* for October 4, 1938, the brochure "Engineering, A Career—A Culture," Programme A, a picture of Robert Fletcher taken in 1933, a picture of Thayer School's Park Street building, a picture of Bissell Hall, and a 1938 Buffalo nickel. A 1938 Jefferson nickel was given a less favored position, perhaps for partisan reasons, in the cement beneath the cornerstone.

During the summer of 1939, the faculty was occupied with the move from Bissell to Cummings in order to ready the new building for use in September. Also during that summer the School operated its surveying session at an out-of-town location for the first time. The Haffenreffer Estate in Canaan Street, New Hampshire, had been donated to the College that year and its use as a location for Thayer School's summer surveying camp seemed ideal, as indeed it proved to be until World War II requirements necessitated that all instruction be given in Hanover. After the war, Cummings Hall was considered a better location for the summer programs and the College subsequently disposed of the Haffenreffer Estate which became the home of Cardigan Mountain School.

Immediately after World War II, it became apparent that the expanded program of the School and the increased enrollment which was anticipated would require additional space, and the construction of two wings was undertaken. These wings more than doubled the size of Cummings Memorial, bringing the total space to over 40,000 square feet.

Cummings, thus enlarged, proved adequate for seventeen years until, in 1964, the expansion of staff, laboratories, experimental equipment, and faculty research activities made additional space essential. The completion of the new Medical School building made it possible to assign Nathan Smith Hall and an adjoining Butler building, to Thayer School use. These buildings were renovated to provide office, classroom, laboratory, research, and shop space for the School's Radiophysics Laboratory. The cost of adapting this additional 10,000 square feet of space was met in large part by a grant from the National Science Foundation.

Even this major addition, however, failed to satisfy the space requirements of the School's expanding program, and in 1967 a temporary structure was erected between the wings of Cummings Memorial. The 6,000-square-foot area provided by this temporary building is used primarily for equipment storage and for study carrels and offices for graduate students.

Thus, in 1970, Thayer School's floor area approximated 60,000 square feet, and the buildings and the land they occupied were carried at a book value of over $660,000—a far cry from the School's 6,000-square-foot first home which Professor Fletcher purchased for $3,000.

Construction was begun in the spring of 1971 on Murdough Center, rising between the Thayer School and the Tuck School at the west end of Tuck Mall. It will be by far the largest and, of course, most costly Thayer School facility. This new center, with physical connections to both schools, will serve not only the two schools but the College as well, providing a home for College and Associated School continuing education programs. The Thayer School and Tuck School libraries will be joined in this new building. Classrooms and an auditorium will also be available for Thayer School, Tuck School, and College use. In addition, a joint Tuck-Thayer computation center will be included with access by teletype to

Dartmouth's Kiewit Center and with various auxiliary computation equipment. The total cost of this multi-use center, including furnishings, is expected to approach $4,500,000. Occupancy is scheduled for 1973.

CHAPTER 3

Robert Fletcher and His Faculty

ROBERT FLETCHER—full professor and director of the Thayer School from age twenty-three until his mandatory retirement at age seventy, Professor Emeritus, member and clerk of the Board of Overseers until his death at age eighty-eight, recipient of Dartmouth's honorary AM, PhD and DSc degrees. Robert Fletcher—Military Academy graduate of the Class of 1868, teacher of fourteen different engineering courses during Thayer School's first year, only full-time member of the faculty for eight of the School's first twelve years. Robert Fletcher, of whom a former student once wrote, "Few can point to a life work of such singleness of purpose or such signal success. But why pile on words? We all love our Bobby—many of us have received our life's inspiration from him."

What kind of man was this one-man faculty? We have seen that the first impression which he made on both President Smith and General Thayer was less than overwhelming. Yet two months after he had joined the Dartmouth faculty, Smith described him in much more enthusiastic terms: "We are *delighted with him* . . . we have been directed to *the man for the place*. . . . Our Professors are much pleased with him. His moral tone is excellent. He is affable, genial, gentlemanly. He gives himself to his work methodically, earnestly and faithfully. And I hear that his pupils—some of whom are keen fellows—think him an accurate & thorough teacher." Smith "had little fear of being obliged unfavorably to modify" his impressions, and during the ensuing sixty-five years his assessment of Fletcher was to be confirmed and reaffirmed many times over by his students, colleagues, and peers.

Fletcher was to leave strong, lasting impressions on generation after generation of students who, reminiscing on their Thayer

School days later, invariably recalled most vividly the quality and influence of *The Professor*. The temptation to include here the full biography which some day should be written of Thayer School's first citizen must be resisted. The recollections which follow have been supplied by some of his former students especially for this book.

His accomplishments as director and teacher almost invariably merged in their minds with his quality as a human being. "His interest," wrote one alumnus, "went beyond the classroom as he stressed personal appearance and warned against the use of alcoholic beverages. His military background showed up in the classroom and yet he was a warm, sympathetic person who could always find time to help students with their problems, whether they were scholastic or personal. He was respected by all and the example he set and the training he gave were helpful to students after graduation in dealing with others. Professor Robert Fletcher had a profound influence on my life."

Another has written, "Known affectionately to the students as 'Bobbie,' he came to the school with the aura of obedience, precision and punctuality of the Point and that aura still exists in the minds of those who knew him. He was an Engineer, Teacher, Disciplinarian and Humanitarian who devoted his whole time to enhance the name of Thayer School and the welfare and health of his students."

Others have called him "outstanding in his contacts with the students" and have spoken of his "cheery word and the sly bit of humor mixed in with his teaching," his "humanistic approach," and his "sage advice." Probably more revealing of his character were his talks to his classes.

One alumnus recalls a bit of his advice to the Class of 1910: "Gentlemen," he said, "remember that the body is like a steam boiler, feed it regularly and rake out the clinkers and you will always be able to get up steam."

Not quite so appreciative of some of his sage advice, one alumnus has written, "Bobby Fletcher was a didactic fussbudget who early each winter would get us all together on a Sunday afternoon and instruct us in what underwear to use for winter. But he was a fine teacher."

Some excerpts from the *Fletcher Memoir* prepared by Dean Garran and Assistant Professor Kimball add to our understanding of the man.

Fully appreciative of the value of technical learning as he was, he nevertheless felt that the greatest value he could give was in the development of high ideals, mental discipline, and an appreciation of human nature. He recognized that the laws of Nature are immutable, and he taught that the greatest folly of Man is disregard for or denial of these laws; but he recognized also that the laws of human behavior are variable. . . . He lived openly and consistently by his own lights, teaching the truth of his convictions by example rather than by the ever less effectual method of insistence. He was a sincerely religious man and rigidly temperate, never permitting himself the relaxing luxury of tobacco, alcohol, or profanity.

Small and slight of stature, he was physically active and energetic. He had great power of concentration and physical stamina, and he was a prodigious worker. Few men could add to . . . the school duties, demanding twelve to sixteen hours work per day . . . the pursuit of intellectual hobbies, active participation in church and public affairs, and a consulting engineering practice.

He designed and supervised the construction of steel bridges across the Connecticut and White Rivers, and of water-works for the Towns of Hanover and Enfield, N.H., and was Consulting Engineer for waterworks and reservoirs in Lebanon, N.H., and in Hartford and Woodstock, Vt. For more than forty years he was President and Engineer of the Hanover Water Company, as well as a member of the New Hampshire State Board of Health, of which he was President until 1934. In the latter capacity he performed great public services, most notably in the development of the tight, free-flowing septic tank. . . . He was in charge of one-half the very extensive survey to determine the New Hampshire-Vermont boundary line, a notorious boundary dispute finally settled by a decision of the United States Supreme Court in 1933.

Throughout his life Director Fletcher contributed freely to technical periodicals and bulletins, and, occasionally, when the spirit moved him and the ignorance of his fellow men seemed too abyssmal, he wrote words of homely wisdom for the public press. Although these contributions covered a wide field of engineering and lay knowledge, including bridge design, water supply engineering, sewage treatment and disposal, geology, surveying, and mechanics, his outstanding work was "A History of the Development of Wooden Bridges," prepared in conjunction with the late Jonathan Parker Snow[1] [a graduate of Thayer School in 1875, Instructor of Civil Engineering 1877–78, and a member of the Board of Overseers 1899–1925]. . . . All the work on this major contribu-

1. Paper No. 1864, *Transactions*, American Society of Civil Engineers, vol. 99, 1934.

tion was carried on after Robert Fletcher had passed the age of eighty-three. . . . [This forty-page treatise, together with over fifty pages of discussion contributed by twenty-five other writers, is recognized as the most complete and authoritative treatment of the subject ever published.]

His hobbies and recreations were of a type consistent with his nature; most men would consider them intellectual pursuits and would perhaps prefer lighter, more trivial, relaxation. One of these hobbies was an intense study of volcanology, both in delving into theoretical and technical causes and effects and in following the sometimes too apparent manifestations of these phenomena. A related hobby was archaeology, and still another was scientific research in the history of the Bible lands, and the development of civilization in all parts of the world.

With respect to his teaching, a former student has written, "Bobbie Fletcher and Eben Holden were great tutors in practical engineering as well as textbook learning." Another remembers "Bobbie Fletcher's first lecture—or rather talk—to us. . . . He said: 'Here we will teach you where to find information and how to use it after you find it. . . . Now when you do graduate we'll give you a diploma or sheepskin, with a degree on it. I want to emphasize that it is not worth a copper. Anyone who pays you, at that time, enough to buy your salt is overpaying. Commencement is just that and if you don't study and learn you won't progress.' "

Of his more technical teaching, an alumnus recalls, "He was a fine teacher—he socked us with mechanics till it ran out of our ears." Another remembers that in 1922 he "was still teaching 'The Method of Least Squares' and still sitting in on occasional courses of others." One who knew him in the middle twenties wrote of him, "But Bobbie Fletcher was something else! I still have somewhere a paper he gave us in which he proved that you can't test a model and expect the prototype to behave the same way—a mistake many have made. And he must have been 75 when he lectured to us."

Actually, he was then seventy-nine and his lecturing days were far from over. He gave at least one or two lectures every year until the very last year of his life. The author was privileged to hear many of these during the late twenties and early thirties. But most vividly he remembers discussing with him, in 1934, the growing use of welding. Since there were no suitable texts available on the subject, this young instructor was preparing mimeographed notes for his class. Expressing a keen interest in the subject, the eighty-seven-year-old professor confessed, "That is a subject which I know very little about but intend to study up on." And he did.

When Dean Marsden wrote to Professor Fletcher's former students in the summer of 1930 that the professor's eighty-third birthday was approaching, no fewer than 140 sent congratulatory letters. The following phrases typify the responses:

> I wish to tell you what an inspiration your constant devotion to the highest engineering and educational ideals has been to me. . . . Engineering attainments without character are of little value. . . . My pleasantest memories . . . are linked with your classes . . . the human interest you gave the subject and the enthusiasm. . . . It is my firm belief that no other teacher of men ever had a more loyal and devoted group of former pupils than yourself.

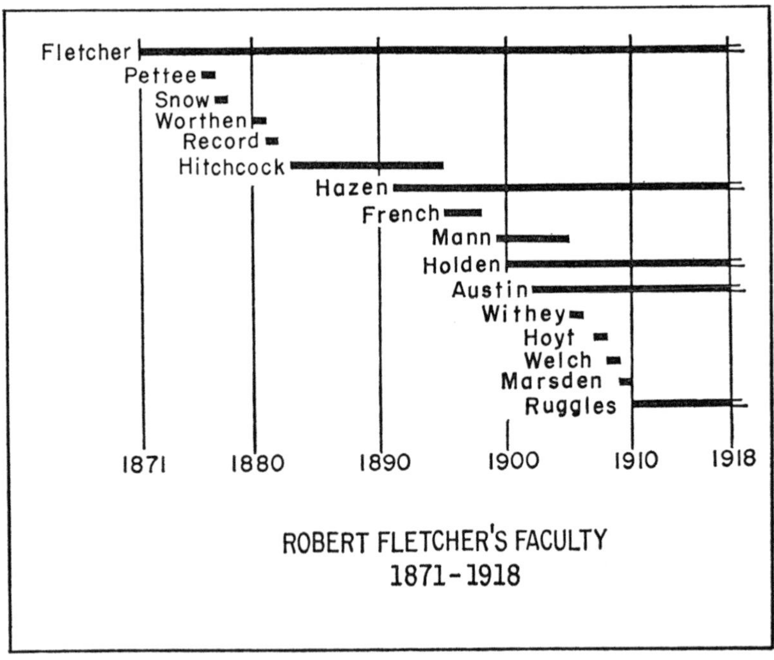

Figure 5

One of Director Fletcher's abilities was to attract able and loyal associates. His faculty was remarkable for its dedication to the School, its devotion to students and to the teaching of students, its small numbers, its long hours, its low pay, and its stability.[2] At no time during Fletcher's regime were there more than four other full-time members of the faculty as shown in the accompanying graph. In all, fifteen instructors served with him, but eight were recruited from immediate or recent graduating classes to fill in for a single year. There were, then, only seven professors with any significant length of service and they were truly remarkable. Of these seven, the three Hs, Hitchcock, Hazen, and Holden, exerted especially great influence on the School and its students between 1883 and 1918.

Hiram Hitchcock '81 joined the faculty two years after graduating from Thayer School and served continuously for twelve years until his death. Except for the last two years, he was the only faculty colleague Fletcher had. Between them, they taught the entire civil engineering curriculum. Hitchcock's annual salary rose from $900 in 1883 to $1,600 in 1894.

John Vose Hazen '76 served from 1893 until his death in 1919. This period showed a major growth in enrollment. The faculty throughout consisted of three to five members, one of whom held only a part-time appointment. Hazen's annual salary reached a peak of $3,200 in 1919. In the long line of teachers to whom the students were devoted, Johnny Vose, as he was affectionately known, was one of the most loved.

"A casual observer," writes one alumnus, "might have classed him as an easy-going individual who would prefer to rest in the shade. Another look at those long legs moving easily over rough terrain would dispel this first conclusion! His eyes never missed anything, not even a rear rodman trying to snatch a little rest under a pine tree. While a hard taskmaster, he had a sense of wry humor that made students think of him as a friend, not as a superior. . . . He not only taught Railroad and Topographical Surveys, he taught students to meet problems under pressure."

Said another, "Johnny Vose, well along in years, amazed us in the field work by the agility with which he threw his long legs over fences, while we clumsily tried to climb over them. He had only one lung and would start a sentence of the lecture, good and strong,

2. No factor, however, during Fletcher's forty-seven years as head of the School had the stability of his own annual salary which stood at $2,500 from 1871 to 1910.

but end up in only a whisper. We all loved him and would do anything for him."

Charles "Ebo" Holden '01 was appointed instructor in 1900. His rank rose abruptly to associate professor during the first five years after graduation and again to full professor three years later. His annual salary rose at a more leisurely pace from $2,000 in 1906 to $2,500 in 1918. He became the School's second director in 1918 and served in that capacity until 1925. Recalled in 1934 from the Mathematics Department, where he had been teaching, he taught in Thayer School for one more year before retiring to emeritus status.

Professor Holden's term as director is the subject of a later chapter. His long career as a teacher, however, was truly noteworthy. Properly addressed by his colleagues as Charles, he soon acquired among his students the label "Eben," or "Ebo," after Irving Bacheller's North Country hero Eben Holden. Although one alumnus refers to "the somewhat austere 'Ebo' image," and another recalls him, perhaps jocularly, as "a conscientious, hard-working nit-wit," he was generally admired and respected. Former students have characterized him as "a brilliant and able man . . . a perfectionist . . . rather high-strung but very capable . . . a bundle of nervous energy that constantly drove, drove, drove to see that each student fulfilled his appointed task . . . possessed of a very fine sense of fairness . . . a very good teacher." "He was very thorough, very serious, a very nervous individual, but withal a very fine Christian gentleman." Many pictures of Holden the professor have remained vivid in his students' minds.

"He was a stickler for accuracy," recalls one, "and taught us the necessity of being precise and accurate. Eben took us on survey parties in the depth of winter . . . when the snow was five feet deep. . . . All of these so-called field curriculum activities helped me immensely in my early engineering assignments before I became involved in administration and executive assignments."

Said another, "All summer we ran a hypothetical railroad over toward Etna. . . . When we quit to eat lunch Prof. Eben Holden . . . used to regale us with lectures on how to be successful. I have a vivid recollection of one such lecture about a man who aspired to become president of the Pennsylvania Railroad so he got a job as a laborer on a section gang but finally became president. With my usual luck, he turned to me and asked my opinion and with my usual taste I told him it was a hell of a way to get to be a railroad president. He looked at me sadly and said, 'Mr. Morse, I am afraid you will never amount to much.' He had a point."[3]

"A familiar sight around Hanover," wrote another alumnus, "was Professor Holden scooting down one hill and up another on a bicycle in order to keep in touch with various survey parties and their instructors. Certainly he had a sense of fair play for on those occasions he always wore a fiery red and white shirt that gave warning of his approach from far away so that no student would be found loafing."

After serving for seven years as director of Thayer School, Professor Holden joined the College Mathematics Department where he successfully combined teaching with community service for nine years. In 1934, he responded to Dean Garran's call to serve the Thayer School again, this time as Professor of Power Engineering, for a one-year term. In 1935, he became Professor Emeritus and he was then able to devote full time to serving the Town of Hanover and the State of New Hampshire until his death on October 12, 1960.

Of the others, Arthur French '92 was a member of the faculty for the shortest term, only three years, but continued his close association with the School throughout his forty years on the Worcester Polytechnic Institute faculty. He was a conscientious and respected member of the Thayer School Board of Overseers from 1925 to 1939. As the author well remembers, degree candidates, who were required to submit to examination by the Board during those years, knew Professor French as the overseer who could ask the most searching questions and demand the most precise replies.

3. Mr. Morse did not become a railroad president but he has had his own highly productive and successful consulting engineering firm for fifty-six years.

CHAPTER 4

The Fletcher Years 1871–1918

BY SEPTEMBER 1871 Thayer School had a professor, a Board of Overseers, a Programme of admission requirements, a curriculum, an endowment, a drawing room, and a recitation room. It also had three students. It was in business.

Within six days of Professor Fletcher's arrival on the Hanover plain on January 17, 1871, he had begun the preparatory instruction of the three students who were to comprise Thayer School's first class: Thomas Greenlay, Henry Hazen, and Albert Porter. They must have learned well, for they were admitted to Thayer School nine months later. Hazen dropped out after completing first-year work, but Greenlay and Porter finished the two-year course to become the first recipients of the School's Civil Engineer degree.

During the spring of 1871, Fletcher, of course, served as General Thayer's personal representative on the Dartmouth campus. The question uppermost in the General's mind was where and how students might prepare for admission to the School. Both he and Fletcher were hopeful, but not optimistic, that Dartmouth might be able to prepare students properly. During his first month at Dartmouth, Professor Fletcher wrote to General Thayer that President Smith "seems to be nearly persuaded that it will be advisable to allow students to omit certain studies during the Junior and Senior college years, so as to devote their time to Mathematics in the Thayer Preparatory Department. Indeed a point was gained at the last faculty meeting, after a stormy discussion. Two students of the Senior class (Hazen and Porter) were allowed to drop German so as to devote more time to mathematics in the Thayer Prep^{y}. Dep't." This helped but did not really make up for the extra work which Fletcher required of them.

By June of that year the Dartmouth faculty had given continued thought to making adjustments. They were considering allowing substitution of work in analytic geometry and mechanics for some Latin and Greek in sophomore year, to be followed in junior year by descriptive geometry and calculus. Professor Fletcher, however, regarded their proposal with some skepticism, saying, "By this arrangement *they* expect to fit their students to enter the Thayer School, and to have no connection with our Prep^{y}. Dep't. I think their success is doubtful, with their present means of instruction."

Thayer, agreeing with Fletcher's view of the College's capability, replied that "The college student who on graduation will be prepared, under the proposed arrangement, to enter upon the curriculum of the Thayer School will be a *rare bird* indeed."

Had the General held a higher opinion than he did of the College's Chandler Scientific Department, he and Professor Fletcher might then have arrived at a satisfactory arrangement. The Department, which had been established twenty years earlier, offered a number of courses both in civil engineering and in preparatory subjects. It was, thus, to some extent in competition with the new civil engineering school, as it was to remain for over eighty years, but, more important, it could perform a valuable service to the School by offering preparatory courses. After this capability was finally acknowledged in the late seventies, the department served the School in this capacity until, in 1959, its function was taken over by the Engineering Science Department.

Thayer had expected that it would require several years for the professor to prepare himself and his school for its opening, and Fletcher was reluctant to launch Programme B as early as the fall of 1871. President Smith, however, was understandably impatient. After all, the 1867–68 College catalog had stated that the School would be opened to students "at the commencement of the next College year." The President prevailed, against the better judgment of both Thayer and Fletcher, in the summer of 1871, and so it was that on September twentieth of that year the professor informed the General, "I have the honor to report that the Thayer School of Civil Engineering has fairly opened."

From that day on, Fletcher bore the brunt of the teaching load as well as the managerial burden of directing the School. His load built up abruptly from the day of his arrival on the campus. After several months devoted to teaching the preparatory class and organizing the School, he taught fourteen different courses during the 1871–72 academic year; the following year, with both Preparatory Department and Curriculum Department courses, he personally conducted thirty-six different courses. Though not every course met every day or extended through an entire term, and though the total student enrollment was only seven, the load must nevertheless have been staggering.

Since about half of his courses were taught in the Preparatory Department, Professor Fletcher was considerably relieved when, at the end of the academic year, the Board of Overseers directed that the department be discontinued. Fletcher's report to the overseers a year later said, "The suspension of the Preparatory Department took a great burden from my shoulders. But the experience of the past year has shown that the load is still too heavy. Four recitations or lectures per day on different topics is too much for one professor, who must prepare himself in each subject by hard study. Add to this the keeping of records and general oversight of the Institution, and the duty cannot be properly done without assistance." The professor of today, with a teaching "load" of six to nine hours per week in one or, at the most, two concurrent subjects, will not disagree with Professor Fletcher's appraisal.

The founder's intention had been that the School should attain "the very first position as an Institution for the training of engineers," should "train only men having a high order of scientific ability, to become ornaments to the profession," and should "prepare the capable and faithful student for the most responsible positions and the most difficult service."

The philosophy of an "essentially postgraduate" professional curriculum is, given this statement of purpose, more clearly reflected in the requisites for admission than in the curriculum itself. Programme A required that, after being examined in English grammar, physical geometry, arithmetic, algebra, geometry, plane and spherical trigonometry, mensuration, surveying, and leveling, the student should study more advanced topics in those subjects plus history, geometrical drawing, descriptive geometry, analytical geometry, the calculus, analytical mechanics, acoustics, "thermotics," optics, magnetism and electricity, chemistry, and astronomy.

General statements of requirements are more revealing of educational philosophy than the specifics. The first Thayer School catalog, published in 1873, advised "Young men . . . not to begin preparation at too early an age, when the mind is not sufficiently matured and prepared to master the advanced studies. Also not to be in haste, at the sacrifice of thoroughness and proficiency. Far better, be slow and sure. Those who can afford it should, for many reasons, avail themselves of the advantages of a course in college or a first-class scientific school, perfecting their preparation, meantime, for the Thayer School. Our best students, thus far, have been such as have graduated at college, or pursued an advanced academic course of study, with the experience of teaching, their age, on entering, being even considerably beyond 20 years."

The 1879 announcement placed more emphasis on college preparation, stating, "It is practicable for young men of sufficient maturity, with limited facilities, to prepare fully, by aid of this guide (Programme A), for the Thayer School. But all persons having Civil Engineering in view, are strongly urged to take a full collegiate course, preferably on a classical but alternatively on a scientific basis, by which, in addition to the knowledge of the special preparatory subjects above named, may be acquired a broader and more liberal training which, as in other professions, so in Civil Engineering, constitutes a preparation of the highest value. To this principle the careers of illustrious engineers bear testimony; and if true in the past, much more will it be emphasized by the severer demands of the future."

The following year, the catalog pointed out that Dartmouth was well equipped to offer appropriate preparation either in its Chandler Scientific School or in its own "Latin-Scientific Course." The latter differed only from the full classical course in the omission of seven term-courses in the Greek language and the substitution of an additional amount of mathematics, science, and modern languages.

Not until 1888 was reference to the possibility of substituting maturity for formal education as an admission requisite omitted from the catalog.

The determination to avoid specialization, which was to remain School policy for the first ninety years, found its first expression in the 1874–75 College catalog where the program is described as "furnishing thorough and systematic instruction in all the fundamental principles and operations pertaining to the science; not to make an 'expert,' at once, in any branch or branches of the profession, but to give the capable student that preparation which shall enable him to become such by subsequent application."

Professor Fletcher enlarged on this statement when he reported to the overseers in 1875:

> Your professor conceives to be the work of the Thayer School, as prepared by the founder and the Overseers, . . . to give the civil engineer an indispensable training which must be fundamental in character, thorough as to principle and general in its scope; practice, suitable in kind and amount, to be combined with theory only so far as necessary for efficient preparation for future service. There must be no attempt to teach the details of a special branch, for what is required, as a basis, is a broad and accurate (although it must be, at first, a somewhat superficial) knowledge of each of the principal branches of the science.

Professor Fletcher strove manfully for over twenty years to develop Programme B, as General Thayer had intended, as the vehicle for carrying out the work of the School. Perhaps his heart was never really in it, for there were few things Fletcher undertook which he did not finish. He probably recognized, as had General Thayer, that the School's curriculum would have to go through a period of Topsy-like growth and that, in order to keep pace with the times, it would have to be continuously reviewed and adjusted. So it was probably just as well that he didn't finish this job. Once a program is set down in printer's ink, it gains a degree of permanence which, in the words of Thayer School Overseer Gordon S. Brown many years later, "makes guideposts into hitching posts." The reverence in which General Thayer, and later Robert Fletcher, were held provided all the guideposts the School needed, even without Programme B.

However, the Thayer School curriculum published in 1879 was presented as a "general scheme . . . based upon . . . the intention of the Founder of the School. . . . This 'Programme B' has been brought . . . to within the last stages of completion." Since it was never brought more nearly to completion, it seems permissible to consider that it was, in fact, Programme B. It was presented in three divisions: Division I, Surveying in General; Division II, Construction in General; and Division III, Special Applications.

Although there is a great deal of similarity, almost to the point of identity, between the program which Mahan had outlined in 1867 and Professor Fletcher's 1879 program, the latter appears to have taken a somewhat narrower and more applied approach and, as indicated by the division titles, to have focused on construction. The single subject included by Fletcher which had not appeared in Mahan's curriculum was Sanitary Engineering.

The rationale can be illustrated by reviewing the presentation of Course I, Bridges and Roofs, selected because it is a subject which dominated civil engineering curricula throughout the first half of the twentieth century. Topics are listed under two categories as primary and secondary. Primary topics are defined as "essentially fundamental, demanding thorough study" and "embracing the curriculum, essentially." They are further sub-divided as "Theory and analysis" and "Practical," each being described as shown below.

Theory and analysis—Textbook and lecture
Regular classroom work.

Analysis of, and deduction and discussion of formulas for, the leading types of bridge and roof trusses.

Theory of suspension bridges. Support and construction of bridge floors. Special applications of graphical statics.

Practical. Only sufficient to elucidate
theory—not to make experts.

Careful inspection and study of works, completed or in progress, by well-arranged tours.

Analyses of existing works.

Bridge projects.

Secondary topics are defined as "topics auxiliary and incidental, as descriptions, experimental data, etc., for reading and reference" which "become a part of professional knowledge only by practice." They are further subdivided as "For the Student" and "For the Practitioner" and described as shown below.

For the Student

(To consult or read about in connection with primary topics. Partly involved in examinations.)

General study of construction of different kinds of bridges.

Centres and false works.

Continuous girders considered comparatively.

Tubular bridges.

General principles of roof construction.

For the Practitioner

(Only to be noticed incidentally and deferred to the emergencies of actual practice.)

Full details of construction. Joints, etc. Methods of erection. Continuous girders, formulas. Tubular, draw, swing and lift bridges, etc. Details of roof construction.

There can be no doubt that the specific subject matter included and the manner in which it was treated changed between 1879 and 1918. It is nevertheless of interest to see the extent to which the 1879 curriculum survived through the forty years that followed its adoption.

1879	1918
Surveying	Theory and Practice of Surveying
Mechanics and General Applications	Mechanics
Resistance of Materials	Mechanics of Materials
Physical and Chemical Properties of Construction Materials	Materials of Engineering
Special Forms of Materials and Structural Elements	Ordinary and Special Structural Work and Operative Details
Bridges and Roofs	Framed Structures
Highways and Railways	Railroads and Transportation
Hydraulic Works	Hydraulic Engineering
Heat and Heat-Engines	Heat, Heat Engines and Power
Sanitary Engineering	Sanitary Engineering
Rivers and Harbors	Canals, Improvements of Rivers and Harbors
Rockwork, Tunneling and Mining	Rockwork, Tunneling and Mining
Not Listed in 1918	*Not Listed in 1879*
Masonry and Foundations	Principles of Electrical Engineering and Applied Electricity
	Business Relations of the Engineer

An alumnus has reminded us that the School's program cannot be fully described, either in 1879 or in 1918, by a list of subjects alone. "One course conducted at Thayer School," he writes, "cannot be found listed in College catalogues. It should be called the Theory of Hard Work. The student left the School building at 8 o'clock for a day's work at some project such as surveying a railroad or topographical survey or measuring the current in the Connecticut. At five he returned to receive an outline of homework that would occupy his evening hours. This might even be topped off by a midnight visit to the plain in front of the School where by lantern light he would set up his transit and train the telescope on 51 Cephei . . . so that he might establish the Azimuth the following morning."

Reminiscing in similar vein, Samuel Hobbs '13 recalls coining a phrase at midnight one Saturday which was later framed as a motto and displayed for many years on a Thayer School wall: "Six days shalt thou labor and on the seventh do the rest."

But curricula and teaching were not Fletcher's only concerns. From the day in 1873 when he noted the limited staff and facilities of the Thayer School in comparison with those of her sister institutions, Fletcher was never to escape the pressures of inadequate finances. They plagued him throughout his directorship, just as they were to plague his successors and, of course, all college administrators. By 1891 financial constraints had become critical and Professor Fletcher urged the overseers to assist in acquiring funds for the School. A printed announcement was thereupon addressed to "friends and patrons of the higher technical education," listing the School's needs as increased compensation for the second instructor—Associate Professor Hiram Hitchcock's salary at that time was $1,200 compared to Fletcher's $2,500 which was apparently considered adequate—; funds for books, periodicals, instruments, and materials; and funds to meet the expense of visiting lecturers and class tours. An immediate increase in endowment of $50,000 was requested but a total of $130,000 was estimated as needed to "make the foundation sufficient for the near future."

"Of secondary importance," continued the appeal, "is the need of means to provide separate and larger quarters,—a modest building—properly adapted to the special needs of the School." The

$1,800 solicited by Professor Hitchcock during the following year, presumably to meet the primary needs listed in the appeal, was applied, instead, to the purchase of the Experiment Station Building which was to become Thayer School's first real home. Thus, not for the last time in the history of higher education, the professor's salary increase was deferred in favor of bricks and mortar.

With the acquisition of a home of its own and the installation the same year of William Jewett Tucker as Dartmouth's new president, attention was next directed to other means for cementing the School's relationship to the College. President Tucker was instrumental in bringing about an abrupt turn in the College's policy toward Thayer School which was to prove highly beneficial to the School from that time forward. This new policy provided that "Students of approved ability and proficiency in the Chandler Scientific Course of the College may elect the first-year courses in the Thayer School for their work of Senior year. At the close of the year they may formally graduate from the College with the degree of B.S. They may then become eligible for the degree of Civil Engineer after pursuing the regular engineering courses of the second-year group."

Thus it became possible for a Dartmouth student to obtain both his College degree and his Thayer School degree in five years rather than in six years as previously required.

The Thayer School, though recommending, had never *insisted* on a college degree as a prerequisite for admission. Therefore, the new policy was a concession on the College's part and a convenience to Dartmouth students rather than, as frequently interpreted, a reduction from six to five years in the formal education required to obtain the Thayer School degree. As the Thayer School catalog accurately stated, "The former short course in engineering, on the Chandler foundation, is enlarged, while the standard of the Thayer School is not lowered. The loss, if any, is to the student who sacrifices the general and liberal courses of the closing academic year in order to save (?) a year for professional study."

The adjustment was in accord with the policy stated by President Tucker in his inaugural address in June of 1893 that "It is always and everywhere the function of the College to give a liberal education, beyond which and out of which the process of specialization may go on in any direction and to any extent. The College must continually adjust itself to make proper connection with every kind of specialized work, not to do it."

The new policy had far-reaching effects. Previously, over forty percent of Thayer School's students had come from other institutions, more than half, incidentally, not from classical but from scientific schools or departments. For the next seventy years, beginning in 1893, almost all came from Dartmouth. Thus, it became the School's primary mission to serve Dartmouth students. The emphasis was not changed until after 1960 when the College Trustees determined to enlarge the graduate school function of all three of Dartmouth's associated schools.

Another, almost immediate, effect of the new policy was a sharp increase in Thayer School enrollment. Prior to 1894, classes had averaged about five students. By 1903, the number had increased to fifteen. It remained at that figure or higher throughout the remainder of the Fletcher Years.

It was presumably not because of the increased enrollment of Dartmouth students that it was found desirable to introduce a new paragraph in the School's 1901 catalog to the effect that "Only young men of correct habits and high character will be accepted or retained. Indulgence of an appetite for intoxicating drink will be sufficient reason for rejection of any applicant;—and such indulgence by an accepted member of the institution during his course will be sufficient cause for summary dismissal." Since Thayer School students had always been subject to College regulations with respect to deportment, the reference to the continuance and dismissal of enrolled students need not have been included. However that may be, the statement remained in the catalog until 1923 when, though continuing to specify correct habits and high character, the need to spell them out was apparently no longer considered necessary. A few years later, even the general reference to moral qualities was deleted.

In the meantime, the educational philosophy, policy, and methodology were being developed. A description of "the indispensable *general qualifications* of the *graduate*" first appeared in the Thayer School catalog of 1902:

He *must* be fairly adept in the routine practice of surveying, so as to hold his place under an exacting chief of party; he must be, at the start, an acceptable junior draughtsman and an accurate computer, able to make a good original, a good tracing, and a blueprint; he must have sufficient practical knowledge of the ordinary materials of construction, gained by adequate manipulations in the laboratory and by good use of available opportunities for observation; he must have facility in making accurate and sufficiently complete records in a well-kept notebook; and the habit and method of keeping himself well-informed as to the progress of engineering science and practice.

It is not here suggested that inculcation of these skills was the School's sole purpose. Enough evidence has been included previously in this chapter to establish the context of higher purpose within which these practical, immediate objectives were to be attained. Nevertheless, few colleges or universities in the 1970s would admit to giving any attention to such mundane accomplishments. The statement remained practically intact in the Thayer School catalog until 1938. The 1910 catalog described some of the methodology by which the purposes of the School were to be accomplished. "Conditions of actual practice are realized as much as possible [with] entire days of unbroken work . . . each subject [being] pursued uninterruptedly to a finish, and usually not more than two subjects . . . under consideration simultaneously. . . ." "Instructors give personal supervision from three to eight hours daily. . . . *The principle of close personal supervision* has always characterized the THAYER SCHOOL."

Laboratory experience, inspection tours to engineering works, and practical work experience were used to supplement classroom study. From the very beginning, frequent examinations, both oral and written, daily recitation participation, and the use of textbooks rather than lectures wherever possible, were the means by which the purposes were to be achieved.

By 1907, the School's need for greatly increased financial resources had become so apparent and so urgent that newly-elected Overseer Otis E. Hovey '89 determined to take a hand himself. Director Fletcher had managed to maintain a precarious balance between annual income and expense, but his ambitions for the School could not be realized within the constraints of his budget. Hovey, therefore, whose deep interest and loyalty were to benefit the School for almost thirty-five years, was determined to obtain a major donation to the School's endowment in order to assist Fletcher to realize his ambitions and initiated preparations for "an attempt to approach a certain individual."

In the course of the next several months, Professor Fletcher assembled a wealth of statistical detail relating to finances and enrollment from 1871 to 1907. He estimated that a total of $200,000 was needed, to be divided equally between permanent endowment and building construction. A few months later, still in pursuance of Hovey's project, Fletcher prepared a "Memorial" to the College Trustees in which he raised a number of pertinent questions. "Does the ownership of the building, now vested in the Trustees, carry any obligation as to present maintenance and further provision of accommodations for the School? Might not the charge for (a) heating, (b) lighting, (c) cleaning, (d) janitor and (e) general repairs be met in the general college expense for 'buildings and grounds'? . . . Does the 'connection' of the Thayer School with the College consist only in the custody of the funds by the Trustees and the provision of accommodations thus far made and no more?" "A certain party," continued the memorial, "who has been asked to provide the greatly needed laboratory building . . . has asked some close questions; and apparently is not inclined to act if he thinks that the Trustees have some legal obligation in the matter to do something on the part of the College. It is rather important to know what is the attitude of the Trustees in this case."

"Our friends tell us," he said, "that we have achieved a good measure of success. . . . Nevertheless, we are ashamed to have our friends come and see our poverty; we cannot conceal from ourselves that we are liable to be left ridiculously in the rear of the procession."

The following spring, the Board of Overseers, taking their position in part at least from the memorial, wrote to the College Trustees, "As it is the sense of this Board that the course of study in the School is a post graduate course of the college, of which the School forms an integral part, we most respectfully request that the Trustees of the College take such steps as they may deem expedient for increasing the endowments of the School to provide for the deficiency in accommodation and equipment." The least step which the overseers sought was the preparation of a statement which could be used in negotiation with Hovey's potential donor. Subsequently, the papers which "the certain individual" required from the College in order to consider the request for a donation to the School were prepared.

It then appeared that Overseer Hovey had aimed high, for the certain individual was identified as Mr. Andrew Carnegie. Finally, three years after the attempt was begun, Hovey had to report to Professor Fletcher and President Nichols that Mr. Carnegie had "decided against assisting the Thayer School in any manner." His reasons were interesting. Considering the College as strictly a college and not a university, he did not believe it should offer, in Hovey's words, "any other courses than the old-fashioned College courses." He believed that, since the School had not grown more than it had in forty years, no engineering school of any considerable size was required in Hanover. He felt that the geographical location of Hanover was unfavorable. In short, he concluded "that General Thayer's attempt to start an engineering school at Dartmouth was unwise and that no effort should be made to perpetuate same."

Disheartening as this result must have been to him, Hovey felt that both because useful understandings had been developed within the College and because the material which had been assembled might be used to approach other possible donors, all the labor had not been lost. Actually, in spite of Hovey's optimism, no single gift approaching the amount requested of Carnegie was to come to the School until fifty years later.

Failing in the effort to attract major donations, the director nevertheless managed to keep the School more or less solvent for the remainder of his tenure by Yankee ingenuity and frugality and with vital assists from the alumni and the College's Amos Tuck Endowment Fund.

General Thayer's intention, heartily concurred in by President Smith and the trustees, had been to make Thayer School financially independent of the College. Dartmouth policy followed this intention closely for over seventy years. Except for a few small gifts from individuals, the School had to meet all expenses from the income of the woefully inadequate Sylvanus Thayer Fund. By the turn of the century, fund income had increased to something over $5,000 per year, but by this time it had become necessary to meet the salary of an additional faculty member and the situation therefore remained tight. Fortunately for the Thayer School exchequer, Professor Hazen's salary was always met from the Chandler Fund although he was, in fact, a regular Thayer School teacher. The cumulative balance of the Thayer School income over expense during this thirty-year period seldom exceeded a few hundred dollars and only occasionally dipped to a deficit of like amount. Whenever a deficit state was reached, it was expected that it would be erased the following year. Until 1912, this was found possible without drawing on College funds.

Other sources of funds were the Thayer Society of Engineers, beginning in 1905, and the Amos Tuck Endowment for Increase of Salaries, beginning in 1912. These two sources contributed $23,000 during the Fletcher Years but by 1918 the debit balance carried from year to year in the College financial statements had accumulated to over $3,000.

Financial difficulties, however, must not be allowed to overshadow Professor Fletcher's accomplishments as the head of the School for forty-seven years. In fact, his successes are the more noteworthy for having been accomplished within those constraints. First and foremost, he and his loyal faculty had provided a civil engineering curriculum which at all times kept pace with civil engineering practice. The admissions policy which developed during the Fletcher Years, requiring three years of broad-based college study, was ahead of the times. Indeed, to the detriment of the engineering profession, it remains ahead of the times to this day. The combination of admissions policy, engineering curriculum, and Fletcher's own philosophy sent Thayer School graduates into the world who made and were to continue to make impressive records of service and accomplishment. During the first thirty years, the number of graduates was not great, totaling less than one hundred, but stimulated by President Tucker's policy in 1892, enrollment increased substantially, and during the last eighteen Fletcher years, 222 Civil Engineer degrees were awarded.

Nor were these graduates out of sight, out of mind. Professor Fletcher kept in close touch with many of them. He always took personal responsibility for a major section of the Thayer School Annual which, in 1918, devoted a hundred pages to alumni affairs.

The address, business connection, and special activities of 513 alumni, including those who had completed only one year at the School, were shown. There were also honor lists of alumni serving the Army or Navy, a record of the twenty-three alumni who visited the school during the year, several pages of articles about alumni whose activities during the year had merited special mention, a summary of the numbers of alumni engaged in various fields of activity, in some cases including the names of especially prominent individuals, and necrologies of alumni who had died during the year.

Professor Fletcher also maintained personal contacts with alumni by attending annual meetings of the Thayer Society of Engineers and by visiting individuals or groups whenever his official travels took him to their vicinities. On one occasion, in 1916, he and Professor Holden took "A circumferential trip around the U.S.A., visiting men of the Thayer School of Civil Engineering and other Dartmouth men." This eight-week trip took them as far south as New Orleans, as far west as San Diego and Vancouver and as far north as Minneapolis, Shawinigan Falls, and Quebec. Their report to President Hopkins says that they "viewed the various environments within which a large number of our 'sons' (47 T.S.C.E. men visited, and 28 College alumni) are working out their problems . . . [and obtained] new points of view, and possibly new points of emphasis in the work of engineering education."

Fletcher's many extracurricular activities contributed indirectly but importantly to the prestige enjoyed by the School in the College, the community, and the world of engineering and education.

But all things must end, and the College's age-seventy retirement policy ended the Fletcher Years in 1918. His brief—for him—statement to the overseers at the time of his retirement said, in part:

It is in order now to say that the task which, by Divine Providence, I have been permitted to fulfill imperfectly so many years is resigned with reluctance, without loss of enthusiasm for the work, and while having apparent strength to go on,—although the latter may be more apparent than real. In fact it has hardly seemed to be a task. The help of assistants and associates, the general attitude of the students, and cooperation of college faculty and Trustees have made the work easy. Especially have the cordial work and assistance to the School rendered by the Thayer Society of Engineers given great encouragement and support during recent years. And I should be remiss if I neglected to acknowledge indebtedness to Prof. Holden in particular during the past ten years or more. His devotion, ability as an instructor and organizer of the work, and good judgment in many ways, have been indispensable since the classes increased in numbers from six or eight to more than twenty.

And so, with the awarding in June of the College's honorary Doctor of Science degree, did Professor Fletcher's forty-seven years as professor and director come to an end.

On January 9, 1936, Robert Fletcher was buried in the "old" cemetery within a few blocks of his lifetime home and even closer to the new home which the Thayer School was to occupy three years later. As Sylvanus Thayer was the Father of The Military Academy, so indeed, in every possible sense, was Robert Fletcher the Father of The Thayer School.

CHAPTER 5

The Holden Years 1918–1925

ALTHOUGH Professor Holden was junior both in age and in length of service to John Vose Hazen, it was he whom Fletcher singled out for special commendation in his brief words of resignation. Also, Professor Hazen was nearing retirement age himself and was not in the best of health. It came as no surprise, therefore, that Professor Holden was named to succeed Fletcher as director in 1918. Under the best of circumstances, the take-over from the man who had so successfully guided the School for so long would have been difficult, and circumstances were far from the best. The country was at war, the College was losing its students to the armed forces, President Hopkins was away from the College much of the time, and Holden himself was deeply involved in organizing and conducting vocational training courses for successive 300-man detachments of enlisted men.

William Montgomery '20 has described the situation.

"Many of the Thayer Class of 1918 who had completed their first year joined the U. S. Coast and Geodetic Survey. . . . When our class of 1919 finished the surveying course it was apparent that most of us would be drafted . . . and we were drafted in the fall of 1917." A ruling was secured from the War Department in December 1917 allowing engineering students to continue their studies while enlisted in the Engineer Reserves. Shortly thereafter, Montgomery recalls, "Special orders came through from Secretary of War Baker requiring all enlisted men who had been engineering students to file application for transfer to the Engineer Reserve Corps in order to complete their engineering studies. . . . Late in April 1918 I returned to Hanover where the staff of military engineers had taken over at Thayer School but they were not ready for us [until] August. We were then put on a course of intensive classroom work from 8 am to 5 pm with heavy assignments for night study and were excused from all military drills and formations. This continued until Armistice Day after which we were discharged."

The new director's personal characteristics and abilities as a teacher have been described in the previous chapter. Like his predecessor, he was a firm believer, with civil engineer John Smeaton (1724–92), that "the abilities of the individual were a debt due to the common stock of public happiness or accommodation."[1] Even while directing the School, he accepted election to the Hanover Board of Selectmen in 1923, a demanding and time-consuming assignment, and in 1924 he was elected a representative in the New Hampshire Legislature. He was to continue a true servant of the public until his death.

His extracurricular activities also included membership in such diverse organizations as the Commission for Conservation of Water Power in New Hampshire, the Sons of the American Revolution, the Corporation of the Mary Hitchcock Memorial Hospital, the Board of the Dartmouth Savings Bank, and the Rotary Club, in addition, of course, to numerous scientific and professional societies.

The return in 1918 and 1919 of students whose Thayer School studies had been interrupted by the war swelled the enrollment for two years but immediately thereafter the number of students dropped abruptly to the lowest level since the 1890s. The next two years were also a time of changeover in the faculty. Professor Hazen's death in 1919 was shortly followed by the resignations of Professors Ruggles and Austin. To replace Professors Hazen and Ruggles, Director Holden found two of his former students, Raymond Robb Marsden '09 and Allen Richmond '15. An electrical engineer graduate of Lafayette College, Harold Lockwood, was found to replace Austin. This faculty continued through Director Holden's term of office.

There was nothing wrong with Director Holden's educational philosophy, academic standards, or moral principles. In all these respects he was a worthy follower of Thayer and Fletcher. His in-

1. *Reports of the late John Smeaton, F.R.S.*, London 1812, vol. 1, p. xxvi.

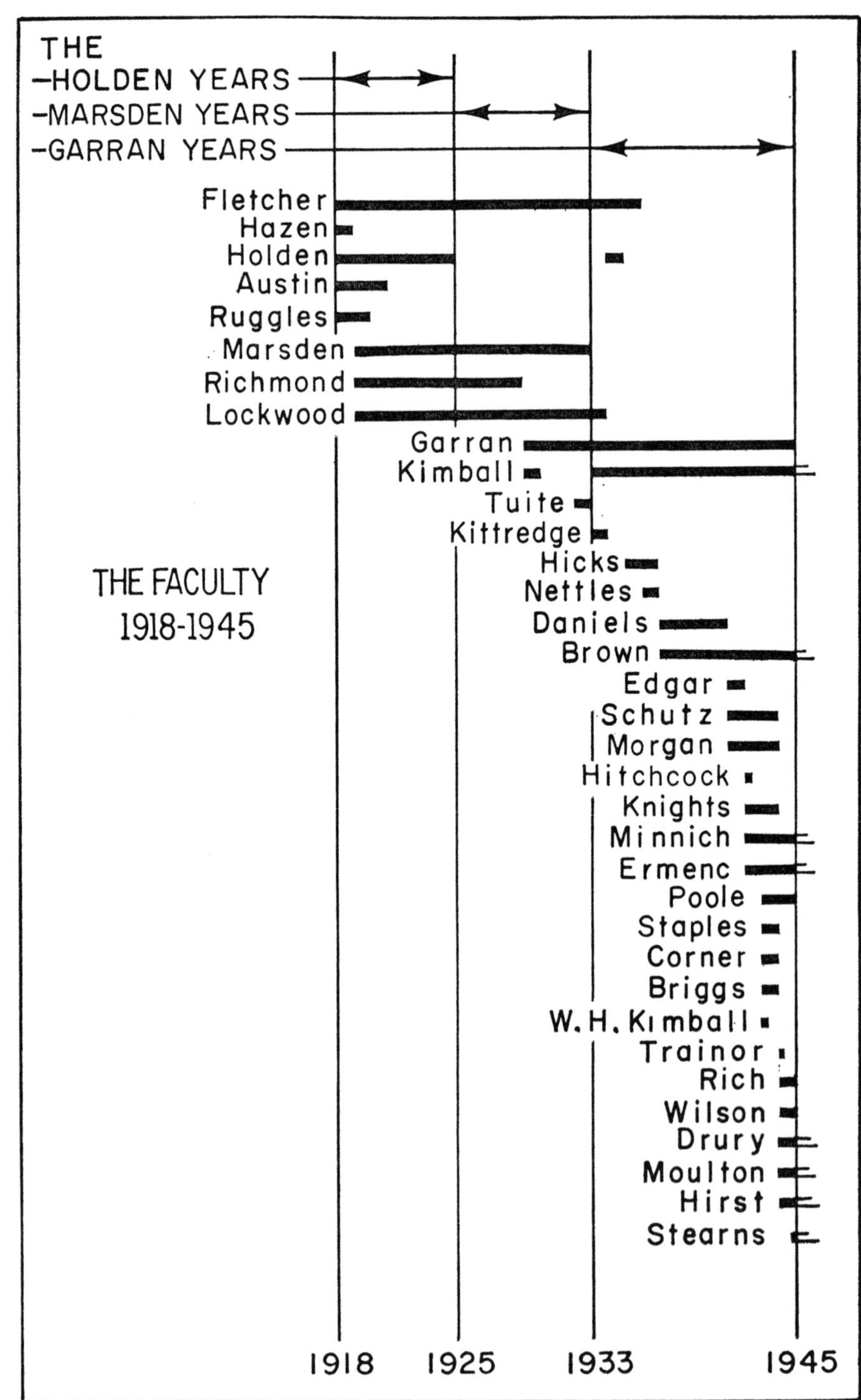
THE
-HOLDEN YEARS
-MARSDEN YEARS
-GARRAN YEARS
Fletcher
Hazen
Holden
Austin
Ruggles
Marsden
Richmond
Lockwood
Garran
Kimball
Tuite
Kittredge
Hicks
Nettles
Daniels
Brown
Edgar
Schutz
Morgan
Hitchcock
Knights
Minnich
Ermenc
Poole
Staples
Corner
Briggs
W. H. Kimball
Trainor
Rich
Wilson
Drury
Moulton
Hirst
Stearns
THE FACULTY
1918-1945
1918
1925
1933
1945

Figure 6

terpretation of educational philosophy was that "the object of all education is to assist in developing and perfecting civilization, and in furnishing the students with an adequate philosophy of life." And, on the academic standards of his School, "The work is set for the best students so that no one, however bright and industrious, can say that he has not indicated to him enough work to utilize his best endeavors."

Although he did not pretend to be defining a profession, as some of his more presumptuous successors were to do, his idealistic view of the engineer was clear in his statement that the engineer should "consider salary and work as two independent problems. He must see to it that he receives enough money to meet his financial obligations, to develop himself and to accumulate a reserve for later life . . . but he must live with the realization that abiding satisfaction comes from accomplishment rather than money."

Director Holden believed that the engineer should equip himself to assist in solving "the industrial problem." "The engineer," he said, "is to be the arbiter between capital and labor and by impartial efforts is to safeguard the rights of each and at the same time those of the public." Matching his action to the words, he brought about in 1922 a cooperative arrangement with the Tuck School whereby Thayer School students were to take work in the Tuck School in business organization and management, marketing, finance, and accounting. Twenty years later, this cooperative arrangement was to lead to the establishment of the Tuck-Thayer curriculum which prospered for fifteen years following World War II. Now the new Murdough Center is a physical manifestation of the continuing common interests of the two Schools.

In retrospect, the largely static curriculum of the Holden Years may seem unimaginative, but it was in keeping with the times. The School's civil engineering tradition, reputation, and emphasis were, however, a handicap to its ability to attract students. No doubt as an effort to reduce the handicap, the 1924 catalog states that the course "is organized to prepare its graduates for activities under the classification of Civil Engineering in its broad scope (older definition) [by which all nonmilitary engineering was called civil engineering] and to include much which under the more recent subdivisions is often listed under other branches of engineering. As a result many of its graduates are engaged in *mechanical* and other than *civil* engineering positions." The catalog continued to emphasize breadth by defining engineering as "the (science and) art of organizing and directing men, and of controlling the forces and materials of nature for the benefit of the human race" and by including in the statement of purpose for the first time "those controlling principles . . . which make a man adaptable so that he can profit 'when improved economic conditions arouse ambition or a new vision makes a change of occupation desirable.' "

These thoughts were not simply expedients to try to increase the dwindling enrollment. They were entirely consistent with the statements made by Professor Holden when he took over the direction of the School in 1918. Nevertheless, the increasing competition of more specialized curricula in other engineering schools, especially the electrical, industrial, and mechanical engineering programs, was to remain a handicap until the Thayer School program was broadened after World War II to include electrical and mechanical engineering and Tuck-Thayer, as well as civil engineering.

In 1920 President Hopkins had written in glowing terms of Holden's "administrative genius" and of the expectation that under his direction Thayer School "would have a well-rounded and an extremely helpful growth." Unfortunately, Dr. Hopkin's expectation was not to be fulfilled. Enrollment fell off and remained low, the physical facilities remained essentially unchanged, the cirriculum continued to include the same courses in much the same arrangement, order, and emphasis as before, and no new activities of special note were undertaken by students or faculty. As might be expected under these circumstances, financing became an even more critical problem as the confidence of the College administration and trustees in the future of the School ebbed.

Although the School's cumulative deficit was carried from year to year as a temporary loan from the College, the amount of the debt was reduced by allocations from the Amos Tuck Endowment amounting to $48,500 between 1918 and 1925, so that at the end of the Holden Years, the School "owed" the College only $6,000. The amount of the Tuck allocations had increased from $2,000 in 1918 to $6,500 in 1920 and to $8,000 in 1922 to 1925.

Concurrently, the Thayer Society of Engineers contributed gifts amounting to about $1,500 per year until the drive of 1925 which raised the gift to $6,750 for that year, a peak which was not again equaled.

The Trustees of the College became increasingly unhappy about the insecurity of the School's financial position and in 1923 appointed a committee to consider "all phases of the problem." The committee's recommendation led the trustees to resolve "that the Trustees feel that they are not justified in meeting an annual deficit in the administration of the Thayer School, and therefore ask the Overseers of the Thayer School and the officers of the Thayer Society what in their judgment should be done."[2]

In reporting this resolution to Thayer Society President Charles Goodrich '06, President Hopkins was careful to explain some of the background, saying that questions had been raised by contributors to the College's Alumni Fund and also by prospective donors to the College about the appropriation of College funds to meet the deficits of the associated schools. He explained that the Tuck endowment was more than adequate to prevent a deficit in the Tuck School budget and that the "apparent" Medical School deficit was, in his view, more than offset by the contribution which that school was making to the health of the faculty, students, and community of Dartmouth and the wider northern New England area. Noting that "the endowment of the [Thayer] school is practically nothing and has never been increased," he recognized that the School's expenses must continually increase "if we are to maintain it under new conditions as an A 1 school, and none of us would be willing to maintain it differently."

Reassuringly, but perhaps not entirely convincingly, he wrote, "Needless to say, no one on the Board of Trustees is willing to consider the possibility of giving up the Thayer School." But he added that "none . . . feel . . . that we can go on continuously maintaining the Thayer School from college funds . . . without some signs of a very largely increased endowment for the Thayer School work."

Director Holden, too, tried to reassure Mr. Goodrich on the basis of an interview which he had had with President Hopkins, saying that "The Trustees do not contemplate precipitate action on their

2. Minutes of Trustees meetings, May 4, 1923.

vote. . . . Ample time will be allowed." Although he realized that, in addition to low endowment, low enrollment was a principal ill of the School, Holden insisted that first-year students should be treated as students in a graduate school rather than as seniors in an undergraduate college in order to "meet the intentions of the founder." There can be no doubt that the enthusiasm of Dartmouth students for Thayer School was considerably lessened by the constraints resulting from this interpretation. For example, no participation was allowed in teams requiring daily practice and extended out-of-town trips. "Students now have three years," explained Holden, "during which they may participate fully in College activities."

The overseers continued to press for increased enrollment. The minutes of their April 1924 meeting expressed confidence that an increase in the enrollment of Thayer School from the present fifteen or twenty to forty or fifty would "involve little or no extra expense; that the School was never before in better condition, as to equipment and its teaching staff, to give the highest grade of training and realize the ideals of its founder."

President Hopkins had explained that the vote of the trustees was "made looking to the long future and that there is no opinion on their part that immediate action should be taken." When asked by the overseers "how far and how long the Trustees of the College would be disposed to continue even a diminishing subsidy," President Hopkins replied that "a period of from two to four years was expected as the time needed to put the School on a wholly self-supporting basis."

This reasonable facsimile of a sword of Damocles hung over the head of Professor Marsden, when, on the resignation of Director Holden, he assumed the deanship of the School in 1925.

FOUNDER AND PROFESSOR, 1871

Sylvanus Thayer
Braintree Historical Society

Robert Fletcher
U. S. Military Academy Archives

SIX DEANS

Portraits: C. A. Holden 1918–25, R. R. Marsden 1925–33, F. W. Garran 1933–45
Seated: W. P. Kimball 1945–61, M. Tribus 1961–69, D. V. Ragone 1970–

OVERSEERS

With President Hopkins, 1935
Standing: A. C. Tozzer, A. W. French, E. J. Morrison
Seated: R. Fletcher, President Hopkins, Dean Garran
Absent: O. E. Hovey

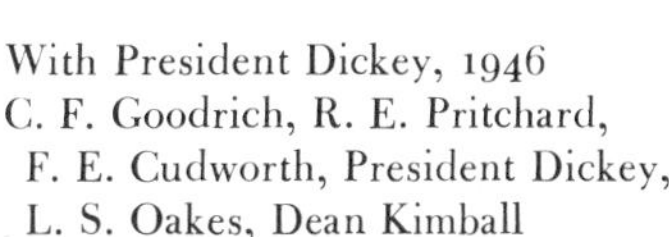

With President Dickey, 1946
C. F. Goodrich, R. E. Pritchard, F. E. Cudworth, President Dickey, L. S. Oakes, Dean Kimball

With President Kemeny, 1971
Standing: H. C. Beck, Jr., W. F. May, R. T. Barr, J. D. Dodd
Seated: J. H. Wakelin, Jr., Dean Ragone, President Kemeny, D. M. Lilly
Absent: G. S. Brown, J. B. Cook, D. N. Frey, J. E. Schlachtenhaufen, Provost Rieser

NINE PROFESSORS

H. A. Hitchcock 1883–95

J. V. Hazen 1891–1919

F. E. Austin 1902–21

M. G. Morgan 1941–44, 1947–

E. A. Sherrard 1946–66

G. A. Taylor 1949–

G. A. Colligan 1962–

A. O. Converse 1963–

B. U. O. Sonnerup 1964–

THAYER SCHOOL FACULTY, 1945

(Portraits: Sylvanus Thayer, Robert Fletcher)
Standing: N. H. Rich, F. R. Drury, J. P. Poole, N. E. Wilson, R. G. Moulton, S. R. Stearns, J. M. Hirst
Seated: J. J. Ermenc, E. S. Brown, Dean Garran, W. P. Kimball, J. H. Minnich

THAYER SCHOOL STUDENTS AND FACULTY, 1871

Professor Fletcher

T. S. Greenlay '73
Photographed 1893

H. A. Hazen '73
Photographed 1889

A. H. Porter '73
Photographed 1892

THAYER SCHOOL STUDENTS AND FACULTY, 1971

Present: 28 students, 19 faculty   Absent: 50 students, 7 faculty

TWO SMALL CLASSES

Professor Fletcher, W. H. Puffer '92, A. W. French '92, J. Walker '93, H. E. Abbott '93, H. A. Symonds '93
Absent: E. J. Morrison '93, S. G. Walker '93

THAYER SCHOOL'S FIRST DOCTORS OF ENGINEERING

T. J. Black '67 and A. Porteous '67
Valley News, West Lebanon, N.H.

Thayer School's Park Street Home, 1892–1912

Thayer School's Bissell Hall Home, 1912–39

Thayer School's Cummings Hall Home, 1939–

Murdough Center, 1973–
Model showing how Center will join Thayer School (in foreground)
with Tuck School (in background)

Classes of 1894 and 1895 at work with Professor Fletcher (at left end of table) and Professor Hazen (right rear)

Classes of 1888 and 1889 with Basic Equipment

Standing: A. W. Hardy '89, T. Flynn '89, W. R. Michie '89, C. H. Cheney '88

Seated: Professor Hitchcock, C. F. Chase '89, F. B. Sanborn '89, H. S. Eaton, '89, O. E. Hovey '89, C. H. Nichols '88, Professor Fletcher

Class of 1909 with Basic Relations

Standing: S. L. Ruggles, A. B. Barnes, R. G. Knight, G. F. Baine, F. S. Weston, W. C. Winkley, P. L. Thompson, F. H. Munkelt, P. W. Stickney, J. H. Stone, R. Hazen, H. O. Rugg, E. A. Lincoln, C. P. Richardson

Seated: E. T. Richards, R. S. Danforth, Professors Holden, Fletcher, Austin, Mr. Welch, R. R. Marsden

Survey Party at Work

E. K. Blanchard '77, Chainman, left

Others (probable): J. A. Worthen '76, Recorder, standing; C. H. Pettee '76, Recorder, seated; M. Moulton '78, Rodman; J. P. Snow '75, Instrumentman, right

Gauging Discharge from "Blow-off" in Vale of Tempe. Professor Fletcher with members of Class of 1897

Bridge Inspection, 1910
Professor Holden, A. W. Wood '11, P. S. Dow '11, H. A. Wells '11, F. S. Hanson, Jr. '11, M. Readey '11

Members of Class of 1942 on Wheels
Fore Rod: J. V. Kelsey; Chauffeur: J. D. Bowe; Instrumentman: R. C. Tousley; Tripod: R. T. Barr; Easy Rider: J. P. Hands; Rear Rod: M. L. Nevius

Professor Austin's Electrical Engineering Laboratory, circa 1915

Professor Hirst's Electrical Engineering Laboratory, 1951
Professor Hirst, C. A. Sherman '52, K. S. Frosig '52, V. D. Macomber '52

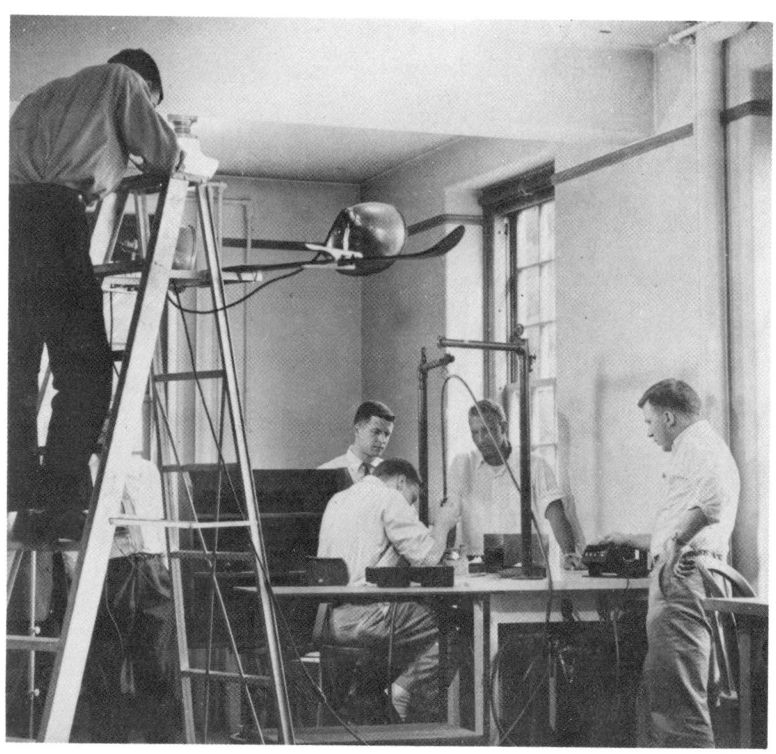

Making Movies of Improved Industrial Techniques
in Work Simplification Laboratory, 1957
On ladder: M. C. Anderson TT'58; Demonstrating: C. W. King, Jr. ME'58; Co-workers: C. A. Schneider, Jr. TT'58, G. W. Johnston ME'58, E. K. Bixby ME'58

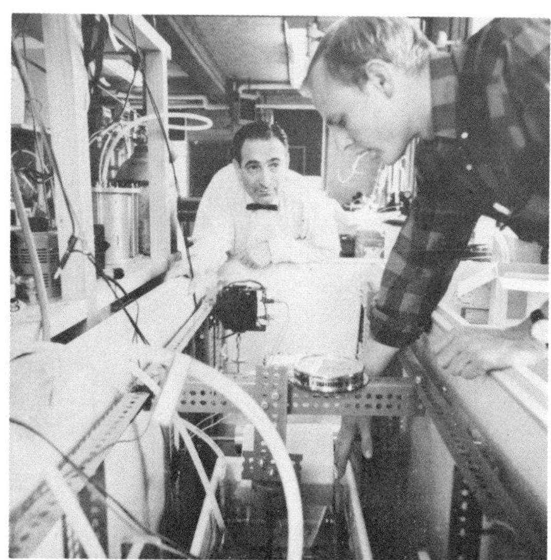

Experimental Reverse Osmosis Equipment
Dean Tribus and C. S. Miller BE'67 ME'68

Thayer School rallies in 1908 with jug of "T.S.C.E. SPIRIT" and other aids for "Power with Capital—No vote for DEBS"

CHAPTER 6

The Marsden Years 1925–1933

As we have seen, the fortunes of the Thayer School were at a low ebb at the beginning of the Marsden Years. Four students were enrolled in second-year work and eight in the first-year class. Because of low enrollment and a deficit budget, no new appointment was made to the faculty with the resignation of Director Holden. The new dean, therefore, was left with only two faculty colleagues: Professor of Power Engineering Harold Lockwood and Assistant Professor of Civil Engineering Allen Richmond '15, as shown in the graph on page 64.

Raymond Robb Marsden, a native of Utica, New York, where he prepared for Dartmouth at the Utica Free Academy, received his Civil Engineer degree from Thayer School in 1909. He remained at Thayer School for a year after graduation as Instructor in Surveying, Stereotomy, and Laboratory. In 1910, he joined the Hardy S. Ferguson '91 firm in New York City as surveyor and designer, where he remained for five years. There followed brief associations as construction and design engineer with the Laurentide Company, Riordan Pulp and Paper Company, and the Atlas Powder Company. In 1919, he became Professor of Civil Engineering under Director Holden, whom he succeeded as head of the School in 1925.

Dean Marsden, himself a product of the Thayer-Fletcher-Holden tradition in engineering education, was in complete sympathy with it and was therefore inclined to hew to the School's long-held philosophies and policies with a minimum of change. That he was successful in this aim is evident in the School's year-to-year progress and in a comparison of the program as it was at the beginning and at the end of the Marsden Years. However, as soon as he accepted the deanship, and even before he occupied the post officially, Marsden, with his faculty and the Board of Overseers, undertook a searching review of the School's program, particularly as it related to that of the College. The results soon became apparent. First, President Hopkins, who had participated in the discussions, issued the following broad statement of policy which was consistent with the School's traditions and at the same time helpful in determining its future:

> The policy of the Thayer School of Civil Engineering is based upon the theory that the purpose of an education is to give a man breadth and depth in his knowledge. In the field of Civil Engineering, therefore, the educated engineer, under the policy of the School, must first of all have acquired the general culture which it is the purpose of a college education to give and must then have superimposed upon this, specialized knowledge in regard to the scope of the field of engineering and the various facts which have to do with basic principles essential to a civil engineer. In other words, it is the purpose of the School to give to the college educated man knowledge of the fundamental theory and practice of engineering, but at the same time to induce him to see the relationship of engineering to life as a whole.

Two adjustments of the School's program were considered to be consistent with this statement of policy and were immediately set in motion: revision of the calendar and rearrangement of the first-year courses.

Until 1925, Thayer School's calendar had been planned with two primary considerations in mind. First, an extended period should be available between the end of first-year work and the beginning of second-year work during which all students might acquire practical experience in engineering work. This was made possible by beginning first-year work in July, just one month after the end of the juniors' second semester so that the year's work could be terminated in mid-April of the following year, freeing an uninterrupted five-month period for employment between mid-April and mid-September. Also, second-year work ended with the granting of the Civil Engineer degree in late April so that graduates might enter employment at the beginning of the construction season rather than two months later when the season would be well under way and jobs might already be filled.

Immediately after the March and April meetings of the Board of Overseers in 1925, the Thayer Society issued a bulletin announcing that "The first year of the Thayer School shall conform to the customs of the Senior year in the College as regards class activities, athletics and social features. . . . This question of having the same calendar year as the College has received the hearty support of a great number of the alumni and it is felt by the President and many members of the faculty of the College that it will increase the number of students who will elect Thayer courses. Many alumni feel that the spring of their Senior year is one of their pleasantest memories."

To implement this decision, the opening of the summer surveying course was deferred to mid-August and field work terminated in time for the opening of the College's fall semester in mid-September. The academic year for the first-year class then extended to the following June, coinciding with the College year and enabling first-year students not only to be on campus throughout senior year but also to receive their bachelor degrees with their class in June. After a transition year, the calendar of the second-year class was also adjusted to coincide with the College year, terminating with the award of the Civil Engineer degree also at the College commencement exercises.

The revision of the calendar was accompanied by the rearrangement of the first-year courses. The class schedule, which had been in effect for both first-year and second-year classes since 1871, consisted of two concurrent courses. Normally, each course continued to completion, whereupon another course would take its place. This arrangement had the advantages of concentration, continuity, and flexibility. Each course continued for just the number of half days which its coverage required, regardless of the calendar of semesters and vacations. However, it had what appeared to be a distinct disadvantage in being out of phase with the two-semester, five-course schedule of the College in which courses were scheduled on Monday-Wednesday-Friday and Tuesday-Thursday-Saturday cycles. After lengthy consideration, the Board of Overseers accepted the faculty's recommendation to fit the first-year courses to the College cycles in order to carry the student's College experience through his senior year and in the expectation that this, too, would stimulate enrollment. In announcing this change, the Thayer Society Bulletin stated that "It is hoped . . . to so rearrange the present curriculum that the first year will be attractive to many Seniors in College who might not wish to take the full five year course. . . . The courses as heretofore laid out have prevented many men in the College from selecting Thayer School courses in conjunction with their College work."

The *intensive*, or *continuous*, arrangement of courses was retained for the second-year class throughout the Marsden Years but was abandoned in 1934 in favor of the *intermittent*, cyclic schedule, on recommendation of Dean Garran and his faculty. It is interesting to note that five years later both first-year and second-year courses returned to the *intensive* schedule until World War II. The plan then became a wartime casualty that was never regained.

Referring to the 1925 readjustments described above, Dean Marsden stated that the keynote was "cooperation and integration." "This change," he said, "has brought forth none but favorable comment, as it enables the first year men to participate in some undergraduate activities from which they were previously debarred. . . ." One of the examples of "cooperation and integration" was the inclusion in the first-year curriculum of a City Planning course offered by the Department of Fine Arts. This particular cooperation was short-lived, however, giving way, after a one-year trial, to two free electives in College departments. These electives, too, had disappeared in favor of engineering courses by 1929.

With respect to curriculum, Dean Marsden explained that, "As the underlying policy of the School has always been to teach the fundamental principles . . . no radical change is to be expected in the subject matter presented." The table on page 52 has shown that twelve of the thirteen courses in the 1879 curriculum survived to 1918. Now we find that nine of the courses which were the same by name or general coverage survived through the Holden Years and the Marsden Years. Two additional courses introduced during the Fletcher Years also survived. A course in Construction Methods was introduced in 1925, and in 1929 the Railroads and Transportation course was replaced by a course in Highway Construction.

Although enrollment increased modestly during the Marsden Years, the three-man faculty continued to provide all the necessary instruction. During this period, too, there was only one change in personnel. In 1929, Assistant Professor Richmond resigned to accept the post of Assistant to the Secretary of the American Society of Civil Engineers in New York. His place was filled by the appointment of Frank W. Garran, a graduate of Norwich University, who had been Professor of Civil Engineering at the College of Charleston, South Carolina. At the same time, in order to fill in during Dean Marsden's leave of absence, William P. Kimball '29 was appointed Assistant in Engineering for the year 1929–1930, thus beginning an association with the Thayer School faculty which was to last more than forty years.

Almost throughout his term of office, Dean Marsden was handicapped by ill health. His leave of absence in 1929–1930 restored him temporarily to good health, but he found it necessary to resign his post in 1933. Apparently fully recovered, he held various public and private engineering positions until 1940 when he returned to the Atlas Powder Company in Wilmington. Two years later, however, cancer set in and he died in March of 1942 at the age of 56.

CHAPTER 7

The Garran Years
1933–1945

FRANK WARREN GARRAN's deanship consisted of two distinct phases: the prewar years from 1933 to 1941 and the war years from 1941 to 1945. The second phase, which ended with his untimely death in September 1945, is described in some detail in chapter 8.

The first phase was characterized by modest but steady growth in the School's program. The second phase saw a quantum jump in the magnitude of the operation and an opportunity, through engagement in the nation's war effort, to make an unprecedented contribution to the welfare of Dartmouth.

In 1933, the staff consisted of three faculty members and one secretary-librarian; in 1945, there were eleven faculty members, two secretaries, and a librarian. In 1933, there were 15 students; in 1945, there were 68, all of whom were enlisted men enrolled full-time in the Navy's V-12 civil engineering curriculum, and an additional 153 Navy Deck Officer candidates were enrolled in one Thayer School course. In 1933, civil engineering was the only curriculum offered; by 1945, mechanical engineering and the Tuck-Thayer curriculum in engineering and business administration had been added, and electrical engineering had been authorized. In 1933 the school was housed in the remodeled 1866 College gymnasium; in 1939 the new Cummings Hall was occupied, and by 1945 preliminary plans were completed for the addition of two wings which would more than double the space. In short, the quality and character of Thayer School's program for many years to come were firmly established by Dean Garran and his faculty before the end of World War II. Concurrence and length of terms of his faculty are shown in the graph on page 64.

Since Dean Garran provided the leadership of the School for twelve crucial years, his qualifications and characteristics are part of the story of the School. Born in Boston in 1894, he received a Bachelor of Science in Civil Engineering degree from Norwich Unversity in 1917 and a Master of Science degree from the Massachusetts Institute of Technology in 1924. In the meantime, he had served for two years in the Army Engineer Corps, had been headmaster of Atkinson Academy in Atkinson, New Hampshire, and an assistant professor of civil engineering at Norwich. After teaching briefly at the University of Arizona and the College of Charleston, South Carolina, he accepted appointment as Assistant Professor of Civil Engineering at Thayer School.

He was on the Board of Trustees of Norwich University from 1934 to the time of his death and was an active member of the American Society of Civil Engineers, the Society for the Promotion of Engineering Education, the Dartmouth Scientific Association, and the Vestry of St. Thomas Church in Hanover.

Although not himself a graduate of a liberal arts college, Dean Garran was a firm believer in a broad cultural background for every engineer. In fact, it was his conviction in the advantages of a liberal education for the professional man which first attracted him to Thayer School. Here he found an opportunity to teach engineering in an environment consistent with his educational beliefs. He also found students who possessed the education and maturity to appreciate the values of the profession which they wished to enter. As dean, he accomplished more fully than had ever been done before, or has yet been done elsewhere, the liaison between liberal arts and engineering education.

He was a tremendously hard worker, inspiring those who worked with him to achieve by equal diligence and perseverance results which they otherwise would have hesitated to attempt. The 1948 Thayer School Register was dedicated to his memory, noting that "With unmitigated selflessness he gave the last sixteen years of his life, as a teacher and administrator, to the highest ideals of engineering education and to the School he loved. His accomplishments in recreating the School of Sylvanus Thayer and Robert Fletcher and in reshaping it for the greatest service to the Country, the Profession and the College are a matter of record."

With the resignations of Dean Marsden and Professor Lockwood, Dean Garran found himself in 1933, like Robert Fletcher in 1871, a one-man faculty. He moved quickly, however, to appoint Clifford P. Kittredge, an MIT mechanical engineering graduate, as Instructor in Power Engineering and to bring William P. Kimball '29 back to the School from his position with a consulting engineering firm in New York City. Thus, by the beginning of the summer session, he had brought the faculty up to full strength. During the next eight years, the power engineering position was held, successively, by Professor Holden, recalled from the Mathematics Department, James Ryan Hicks, a Georgia Tech mechanical engineering graduate with graduate study and teaching experience at Columbia, and Arthur Noyes Daniels, a Naval Academy graduate with a master's degree in mechanical engineering from Harvard.

The faculty was increased by thirty-three percent in 1936 with the appointment of Hill R. Nettles as Instructor in Civil Engineering. He was replaced the following year by Edward S. Brown '35 who had earned a master's degree in sanitary engineering at Harvard. In 1941 Professor Daniels was called to active duty in the Navy and was replaced by Millett G. Morgan, a Cornell electrical engineering graduate. The faculty was further increased by the addition in 1941 of Kenneth K. Edgar whose master's degree in industrial engineering from Ohio State University enabled him to provide special instruction to Tuck-Thayer students. Thus Thayer School entered World War II with five full-time faculty members.

Dean Garran was an outstanding teacher and subscribed readily to the long-standing tradition of the Thayer School as an institution whose faculty was primarily and almost exclusively dedicated to teaching and whose students were primarily, if not quite so exclusively, dedicated to learning. He conceived the School's mission as an Associated School of Dartmouth College to be, quite simply, to serve those Dartmouth students who wished to become civil engineers. In the 1930s, the College's program, apart from its associated schools, was devoted exclusively to undergraduate liberal education. The associated schools were expected to serve Dartmouth students rather than to attract graduates of other institutions. Professional education in medicine, engineering, and business, based on and integrated with the College's undergraduate program, was acceptable. Out-and-out graduate study was not. With few exceptions, research was viewed as irrelevant unless it was an integral part of a formal classroom or laboratory course.

If this rather limited concept of higher education was acceptable in the humanities, social sciences, and natural and physical sciences, it was at least as acceptable in engineering. The man who held a bachelor's, or "first professional," degree in engineering was considered to have completed his formal education and to be fully prepared to embark on his professional career. In this setting, Dean Garran and his faculty set about to provide their students with the best possible preparation for a civil engineering career.

They did not accept the prevailing philosophy that the engineering student's education should consist almost entirely of science and engineering studies. On the contrary, they outdid their predecessors in emphasizing the value of the liberal arts preparation which three years in Dartmouth College gave their students. They did, however, accept the prevailing philosophy that the engineering graduate should possess the tools of his trade and be prepared to be productive immediately on graduation. As Dean Garran advised his faculty, "Engineering is alive and real. We should make it that way in our teaching. If a single student finishes a course in a fundamental subject without being aware of its applications to engineering work or without confidence that he can apply what he has learned to a useful purpose, I feel that we as teachers have failed." While accepting this pragmatic view, the faculty, at the same time, considered their mission to be the preparation of students for a long lifetime of engineering, not just for the first years after graduation. Accordingly the 1939 catalog substituted for the traditional statement of "the indispensable general qualifications of the graduate," the more farsighted statement that "The purpose is to restrict the work of instruction chiefly to those fundamental principles, methods and operations basic to engineering. By this method the student is efficiently equipped to undertake the work which will be allotted to him during early years of practice and at the same time is trained to grasp the concepts which form the groundwork of advanced and original work required to attain eminence in his technical field."

Dean Garran had been well pleased to inherit the School's traditional five-year program consisting, as it had since 1892, of three years in Dartmouth followed by two years in Thayer School. But neither he nor the members of his faculty were willing to settle for the status quo. The shape of things to come in engineering education was just beginning to emerge in the prewar years. With one eye toward that future and with another eye toward attracting more students to first-year work, a substantial reshuffling of courses between first and second year took place. Basically, this involved placing most of the courses later to become identified as engineering sciences in the first year and placing the more applied, civil-engineering-oriented courses in the second year. For example, the basic electrical engineering course and the broad engineering law course were moved into the first-year program and the courses in highways, construction methods, and water supply and sanitation, into the second year.

Another development which kept Thayer School in the forefront of engineering education was a modest increase in breadth and a change in emphasis in those engineering sciences not specifically related to civil engineering. The prerequisites were also in keeping with the best curricula of the time. They included, in addition to humanities and social science courses, four courses in mathematics, four in physics, two in chemistry, and one in surveying. The prerequisites in graphics were reduced from four courses to three.

The curriculum still contained most of the courses which had first appeared in 1873, though the approach and treatment of subject matter within the courses had changed vastly with the development of the sciences on which they were based and the art by which they were applied. An example of such a change was the adoption of the soil mechanics approach to foundation engineering.

Both the reshuffling of courses and the broadening of the engineering science base served the interests of Dartmouth students heading for some branch of engineering other than civil. The adjustments made in 1925 had been in the right direction but had not gone far enough. The Thayer School had traditionally emphasized the virtue of "intensive instruction under close personal supervision" made possible by limiting enrollment. However, since World War I, enrollment had been much lower than was necessary to accomplish the desired objective of close personal supervision. This low enrollment constituted a major handicap throughout the entire period between the wars. Enrollment figures revealed two faults: too few students were attracted to Thayer School; and of those who came, too few chose to continue beyond first-year work.

The first of these faults could be attributed in considerable part to factors outside the control of the School, chiefly, of course, the economic depression which had thrown many engineers out of work. Engineering, which had been riding high for many years, was suddenly found to be as vulnerable as other professions to job shortages and wage reductions. Consequently, nationwide engineering enrollments fell off sharply during the 1930s, and Thayer School was actually less affected by the depression than most schools.

The decrease in enrollment between first year and second year may have been due in part to these same external causes. However, the faculty believed that it probably also reflected a growing interest among Dartmouth students in other branches of engineering. The single-minded civil engineering curriculum which had carried the School successfully through its first half century seemed no longer to be viable. Therefore, in order to appeal to students who might choose to transfer after senior year to another engineering school for instruction in other engineering specialties, the 1939 catalog stressed the student's opportunity to terminate his Thayer School work with Dartmouth's AB degree at the end of four years.

In the meantime, President Hopkins had planted a seed which was to grow into a major expansion of the School's program. "In considering the future of the Thayer School," he said, "I become more and more convinced that there would be advantage to the School in a closer relationship with the Tuck School by which possibly in the course of time there might be more joint courses available to both schools." This thinking led promptly to the establishment of "a five-year course in liberal arts and the fundamentals of engineering coordinated and combined with a training in business administration, consisting of three years in the College followed by two years in the Thayer School and Tuck School and leading to the degrees of A.B. and M.S.," later to become known as Tuck-Thayer.

The purpose of the new curriculum was to prepare its graduates for eventual administrative work in any of a wide variety of fields in which the principles of both engineering and business administration are applied. Elective courses offered an opportunity for the student to focus on a specific field or line of activity in which he was most interested without, however, permitting a degree of specialization which would result in limiting his career choice.

The objectives of the engineering and business administration curriculum provided new stimulus toward a broader coverage of engineering than the civil engineering curriculum alone could provide. The faculty recognized that the additional electrical and mechanical engineering was a practical necessity for the success of the combined curriculum. Coincidentally, the additions would greatly strengthen the entire engineering program and might well reduce the first-year to second-year attrition which had developed.

Accordingly, the name of the School was changed in 1941 from Thayer School of *Civil* Engineering to Thayer School of Engineering, and plans were immediately instituted to offer electrical engineering and mechanical engineering curricula to supplement the traditional civil engineering curriculum. Thanks to the curriculum changes that had been adopted during the immediate prewar years, the broader coverage could be accomplished with relatively minor course additions and rearrangements. The program presented to overseers for approval in 1944 and authorized by the trustees in 1945 retained ten courses which had been included in the prewar civil engineering curriculum as the first-year curriculum for all students regardless of their choice of branch. The more specialized civil engineering courses were, of course, retained. Separate second-year curricula were added for electrical engineering and mechanical engineering students. Tuck-Thayer students were to take certain required courses in both schools and to elect additional courses from the offerings of the two schools in accordance with their individual interests and career objectives. This proposal formed the basis on which the School was developed throughout the first ten postwar years.

Neither the World War II activities nor the expanded postwar program could possibly have been accommodated in Bissell Hall. The 1939 move to Cummings Memorial was therefore far more timely and essential than could have been foreseen. It did also encourage the closer ties with Tuck School which President Hopkins had urged and, subsequently, made it possible to clear the ground for Hopkins Center.

The seventeen students and four faculty members who moved gratefully into Cummings Memorial in 1939 found the new classrooms, laboratories, library, and offices spacious indeed in comparison to the outdated and cramped quarters of Bissell Hall. Three years later, the new quarters were bulging at the seams with fifty-five students, a seven-man faculty and a vastly expanded wartime program.

The great improvement in the state of the School during the Garran Years was recognized by President Hopkins in 1945 when he wrote, "In the long and distinguished history of the Thayer School, I do not think that things related to the School have ever been in better condition than at the present day. Whether in the administrative direction of the School, or its organization, the auspices are altogether favorable. Blessed with a capable and cooperative faculty, with more adequate quarters than ever before and with more ample facilities, the School faces the overwhelming demands of the future under conditions as favorable as could be wished for it except for its lack of endowment. It seems to me that the faith of those who have conceived and developed its policies and of those who have undergone its discipline and from their position of importance in the outside world have supported it with their confidence is being abundantly justified."

CHAPTER 8

Thayer School at War 1941–1945

BY PROFESSOR EDWARD STICKNEY BROWN

THAYER SCHOOL's involvement in the war effort may be said to have begun in the fall of 1940 when the U. S. Department of Education voiced a deep concern for the need of special training courses for personnel in defense industries. This came at a time when the fate of Europe lay in gravest peril. France had fallen and the Battle of Britain had just begun as Nazi Germany spread its military might over Europe, North Africa, and the Atlantic Ocean. In this country, the industrial potential was being marshaled to provide the materials of war, and the colleges were populated with uneasy young men faced with the prospect of the lowering of the draft age to eighteen, with the result that induction into the armed services was a daily expectation and a constant threat.

Eventually, the School's role during the war years appeared in two major efforts: first, in the teaching of special courses to serve the needs of defense industries in the Upper Valley area; and later, in Dartmouth's Navy V-12 Program. These were challenging and dramatic roles which were to have a vital influence upon the development of the School during the next twenty-five years.

The earliest defense training course conducted under the supervision of Dean Garran was the Civilian Pilot Training program begun in the fall of 1940. Ground instruction was given at Thayer School by Dartmouth's Professor of Astronomy Richard Goddard and by Instructor Howard V. Lane of the White River Junction airfield where flight instruction was also given by Mr. Lane. The purpose of this program was to prepare trainees for service in air branches of the armed services. Its value was asserted early in the program by the Civil Aeronautics Administration's figures that out of one hundred men who went to Army flying schools only eight who had had Civilian Pilot Training washed out compared with forty who had not had the benefit of this preliminary training.

Between the fall of 1940 and the summer of 1942, when the direction of the program was turned over to others in order to allow Thayer School to concentrate on other defense training programs, well over one hundred Dartmouth students had completed the course of training and entered the armed forces.

In the meantime, beginning in May 1941, the School had begun to offer training courses to serve civilian government and defense industry workers. The first was a special course in surveying to serve the needs of the U. S. Engineers' Office, then located in Lebanon. By July of that year, more courses were offered in engineering drawing and mathematics for defense industry workers. The courses were taught in the Lebanon and Hanover high schools and this program was named Engineering Defense Training (EDT). By October 1941, science and management courses had been added and the title of the program had been changed to Engineering, Science and Management Defense Training (ESMDT). As the importance of these training courses was recognized, the demand for them burgeoned in the industrial centers of Claremont, New Hampshire, and Windsor and Springfield, Vermont. Following the formal entry of the United States into the great conflict, the title of the program, in the interest of accuracy, was changed in July 1942 to Engineering, Science and Management War Training (ESMWT). The courses in these programs were finally terminated in June 1943, when it became apparent that the critical needs of the local defense industries had been largely met and when, because of gasoline and tire rationing, it had become increasingly difficult to travel.

The implementation of these training programs had involved the entire Thayer School faculty as well as others from Dartmouth. Representing the Thayer faculty, Professors Morgan, Ermenc, Kimball, Schutz, Edgar, Knights, and Brown had taught more than twenty courses in the programs. All of the courses were presented off campus and consisted of twenty three-hour evening sessions per course. Guidance and overall responsibility for the courses were in the hands of Dean Garran. The magnitude of the service performed is reflected by the total enrollment of over 1,000 students to whom 573 certificates of successful completion were awarded.

During the 1941–43 period, when the Defense and War Training Programs were conducted by Thayer School, the military picture was affecting the undergraduate situation at Dartmouth. All able-bodied students and younger faculty were liable for immediate induction, and four uninterrupted years of study at Dartmouth became a rapidly vanishing possibility. In the fall of 1942, students liable for induction were offered the chance to enlist in various Naval Reserve programs. Those enrolling in the V-5 program were immediately assigned to a flight school. Enrollment in the V-7 program was limited to selected juniors or seniors for whom induction might be postponed for up to two years. The V-1 program was open to freshmen and sophomores who, by passing qualifying examinations, might be permitted to complete their college education before induction. Since the net effect of these reserve enlistments was the elimination of any possibility of graduate work, the prospect of a fifth-year class at Thayer School was negligible.

Then, in late 1942, with the United States now involved in wars on three continents and on all the oceans of the world, the armed services became disenchanted with the various reserve programs because of their deferment provisions. The Navy decided to supersede its V-5, V-1, and V-7 programs with a single program. Under this plan, all men in the program would be enlisted personnel of the Navy and Marine Corps and subject to all the regulations of these services.

Classes in the V-12 program opened in July 1943. The enlisted men in the program were required to maintain military deportment at all times. For example, students were permitted to be seated or to rise in lecture halls only on command of their leader. In contrast to the earlier reserve programs, there were relatively few participating schools, but each unit was comparatively large. On a given campus, the unit had somewhat the status of an associated school.

Exploratory conferences with the services relative to the setting of a V-12 unit at Dartmouth were begun in 1942 and culminated in a conference in the spring of 1943 at which time the final decision was to be made. This meeting did not lack for drama and may well have been one of the most important meetings in the history of the College and the Thayer School. The last remaining question on the part of the services as to the feasibility of establishing a V-12 program at Hanover was the capacity of the College to handle large numbers of men in the engineering laboratories. Dean Garran and Professor Ermenc attended this crucial meeting in the office of President Hopkins. The critical moment came when the negotiating officer for the United States Navy asked if the Thayer School could handle as many as 200 men per term in the heat power laboratories. Receiving a nod of assurance from Ermenc, Dean Garran replied, "Yes," and Dartmouth was on its way to becoming the largest V-12 unit in the country. The courage and the faith involved in this reply by the Thayer School to the needs of the College and the Navy may be appreciated when it is realized that, at that moment, the School had no such laboratory nor any equipment to furnish it. Furthermore, the School's total plant at that time consisted of only the present central building. The steam power laboratory for the course was set up in the College power plant.

Immediately following the decision to bring a V-12 unit to Dartmouth, the College set about making adjustments to shift to a three-term system, sixteen weeks per term, and making provisions for the influx of some 2,000 enlisted men and the officer staff. At the Thayer School, immediate efforts were made to round up and install necessary laboratory equipment and to enlarge the teaching faculty to handle this enormous increase in demand on the facilities of the School. The countryside was searched, and such useful items as a marine engine, a used gasoline engine, an old steam engine, and a diesel engine were acquired and installed in any available space in the building, such as in the hydraulics and materials testing laboratory. Discarded direct-current motors from the College were converted to dynamometers to load the salvaged engines. A laboratory for compressible fluid flow was quickly set up in the third-floor corridor, the previous domain of the Nigger Island and Pompanoosuc (model) Railroad, by now defunct since its engineers and dispatchers had all gone to war. The storage room at the north end of the attic became a metallurgical laboratory equipped with items remaining from the Defense and War Training Programs. Ready or not, classes for the V-12 program at Dartmouth opened in July 1943.

After two years of continuous and successful operation of this program, an atomic device was exploded over another theatre of the war, and Dartmouth and Thayer School began to retool for peace. About a hundred full-time civil engineering students had been enrolled in Thayer School and more than twelve hundred other V-12 students had been enrolled in the Elementary Heat Power and Electrical Engineering courses specified by the Navy and conducted by Thayer School's suddenly and temporarily expanded faculty in its equally suddenly acquired but somewhat less temporary laboratories.

No one could regret the ending of the war, nor the ending of the Navy's V-12 round-the-clock, round-the-calendar operation. Nor need any one make apology for the part which Dartmouth and Thayer School, under President Hopkins and Dean Garran, had taken in the war. Dartmouth's Dean E. Gordon Bill expressed the belief of many, after Dean Garran's death in September 1945, that he had, in truth, been one of Dartmouth's casualties of World War II.

CHAPTER 9

The Kimball Years 1945–1961

BY PROFESSOR JOSEPH JOHN ERMENC

THE KIMBALL YEARS were a period of revolutionary change in the the history of the Thayer School. It was a period of expansion followed closely by a period of drastic reformation of curriculum structure and course content. Yet the original idea of engineering education at Dartmouth was respected: that a liberal arts education should precede professional training.

The principal figure in these developments which brought the Thayer School into the front ranks of American engineering education was Dean William P. Kimball '29, now Professor-Emeritus, who in his personal relations spans the entire history of the Thayer School. He was a colleague of Director Emeritus Robert Fletcher and of every Thayer School dean since Fletcher.

The period of expansion took place shortly after World War II when the deanship came to Professor Kimball. A few indicators of the growth during the Kimball Years and the people who brought it about are shown in the table below and the graph on the next page.

Year	*Number of Courses Offered*	*Number of Faculty*	*Number of Staff*	*Annual Budget*	*Total Number of Thayer Graduates*
1945	30	8	2	$58,000	
THE KIMBALL YEARS					426
1961	48	18	10	$410,000	

By 1946, curricula of mechanical and electrical engineering were added to those offered in civil engineering and the comparatively new business administration–engineering curriculum. The traditional pattern of three years in Dartmouth College and two years in the Thayer School was maintained.

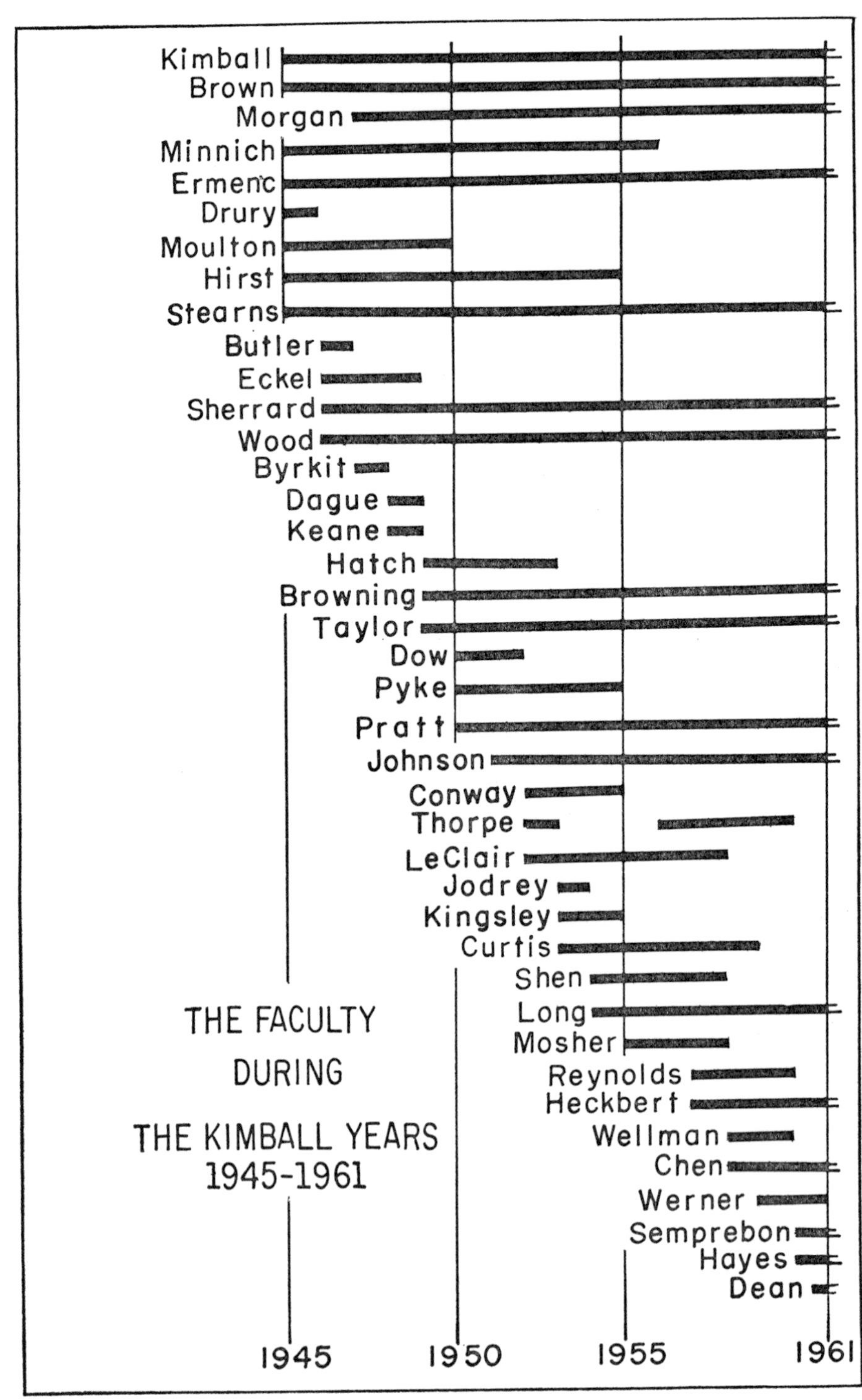
Kimball
Brown
Morgan
Minnich
Ermenc
Drury
Moulton
Hirst
Stearns
Butler
Eckel
Sherrard
Wood
Byrkit
Dague
Keane
Hatch
Browning
Taylor
Dow
Pyke
Pratt
Johnson
Conway
Thorpe
LeClair
Jodrey
Kingsley
Curtis
Shen
Long
Mosher
Reynolds
Heckbert
Wellman
Chen
Werner
Semprebon
Hayes
Dean
THE FACULTY
DURING
THE KIMBALL YEARS
1945-1961
1945
1950
1955
1961

Figure 7

To accommodate the extra classrooms, offices, and laboratories needed, the two wings were added to the Horace S. Cummings Memorial building by 1947. This was especially satisfying to the Thayer School faculty since it was the first construction on the Dartmouth campus authorized by the Board of Trustees of Dartmouth College after the war. This unusual priority appeared to be in recognition of the important part taken by the Thayer faculty during World War II.

The new and old curricula followed the prewar educational pattern of a fixed curriculum. In general, engineering courses were being changed in evolutionary fashion with greater emphasis on more sophisticated mathematical analysis and less on the practice of engineering.

In the mechanical engineering curriculum the conventional shop-training courses in metal cutting, welding, forging, and pattern-making—the vestigial remains of the accommodation of engineering schools to the early phases of the Industrial Revolution in the United States—were completely eliminated and replaced with a four-week summer session devoted to quantitative investigations into the nature of new and old manufacturing processes. Laboratory work, instead of being oriented toward the disciplines of formal tests and report writing, began to shift toward the informal, less structured goal of developing initiative in experimental work of interest to the student. Similar changes appeared in the other curricula.

An encouraging but natural consequence of the Thayer expansion was that at the beginning of the school year about 150 Dartmouth freshmen would indicate some degree of interest in Thayer School. But the somewhat discouraging result was that not more than one-fourth followed through to graduate from Thayer School. Much time was spent by individuals and faculty committees in searching out and trying to rectify the deterrents but, in the end, one generally came to the realization that engineering studies were considered a tough, demanding lot and it seemed that the majority of engineering-interested Dartmouth students did not choose "to scorn delights and live laborious days." Nevertheless, many ways of trying to increase the number of Thayer School graduates were suggested, including the establishment of a "satellite" arrangement with such liberal arts colleges as Middlebury and Bowdoin, though none were adopted for the ostensible reason that such transfer students would have primary "loyalties" toward the institution of their matriculation.

By the beginning of the 1950s, the Thayer School had shed its wartime educational responsibilities and had the new curricula functioning normally but in an atmosphere of uneasiness which pervaded engineering schools throughout the country.

Scientists and mathematicians returning to college campuses from their wartime work on such unprecedented technological achievements as the atomic bomb, radar, the proximity fuse, and the computer tended to denigrate engineering. Dr. Frank Jewett (1879–1949), Director of the Bell Telephone Laboratories, had written a Dartmouth colleague that these achievements had demonstrated that engineering was an anachronism and that its work could better be done by scientists. Dr. Harold Urey, the Nobel Laureate in Physics who had worked in the atomic bomb project, was fond of declaring that the difference between science and engineering was about twenty years.

For the historian all this recalled Helmholtz's industrial reform movement in Germany toward the end of the nineteenth century based upon his slogan "Science is the best technology."

Such comments generally put engineering educators on the defensive and stimulated a reform movement within engineering education throughout the country. It came to focus in the American Society for Engineering Education's Grinter Report of 1955 which evaluated the state of engineering education in the United States and without equivocation recommended its reformation. It stressed the need for greater inputs of science and mathematics into the engineering curriculum as a whole as well as into the engineering courses themselves. Indeed it was suggested that the corpus of upgraded analytical engineering courses, common to all engineering curricula, be called the "engineering sciences." To many engineering professors, especially those who also carried on a private practice of engineering, this was an extremely disconcerting development since it represented a de-emphasis of the art of engineering. More pressure for the reformation of engineering education was generated by the unexpected and unsettling Russian successes in producing the atomic bomb (1949), the hydrogen bomb (1953), and of course, later, Sputnik (1957).

With this background the Planning Committee of the Board of Trustees of Dartmouth College established an ad hoc committee in 1954 to evaluate engineering education at Dartmouth. The members of this committee were Gordon Stanley Brown, Solomon Cady Hollister, and John Alister Hutcheson. Doctor Hollister had been President of the American Society for Engineering Education and recipient of its highest honor, the Lamme Award, and, after a distinguished career as engineer and educator at other institutions, had become Cornell's Dean of Engineering. In this post, he was largely responsible for the adoption of the five-year curriculum by Cornell's College of Engineering and for the remarkable multi-million-dollar expansion and development of that college's engineering plant in which ten major new buildings were constructed. Dr. Hutcheson's career had been with the Westinghouse Corporation where he worked successively in radio and television departments, had been Vice President for Research and Development, and was now Vice President for Engineering. From this background, he was able to provide solid, thoughtful appraisals of engineering education's past and potential future service to industry. Dr. Brown had received the George Westinghouse Award as the year's outstanding younger teacher at the annual meeting of the American Society for Engineering Education held at Dartmouth in 1952. He was head of MIT's Electrical Engineering Department, later to become MIT's Dean of Engineering and, still later, Dugald C. Jackson Professor of Electrical Engineering. Dartmouth, too, was to recognize him, first by membership on Thayer School's Board of Overseers and later by the award of its honorary Doctor of Science degree.

In order to implement the ad hoc committee's recommendations, President Dickey appointed an interdepartmental committee, under the chairmanship of Provost Donald Morrison, consisting of Dean Kimball, Thayer School Professors Browning and Morgan, Mathematics Professors Kemeny and McCarthy, Physics Professors Sears and Rieser, and Chemistry Professor Wolfenden. It soon became clear that the Grinter Report was to be the pattern for change.

This remarkable changeover, in which Dean Kimball had been the leading figure, was completed by 1958. What emerged from four years of work by many Thayer-Dartmouth committees was unique in American education. It was the creation of a new department within a liberal arts college staffed by an engineering faculty: the Engineering Science Department within the Science Division of Dartmouth College.

The pattern of Dartmouth engineering education was changed from "3-2" to "4-1": four years in the liberal arts College and one year in the Thayer School.

It was hoped that this closer organizational relationship would promote closer liaisons between the engineering faculty and the science faculties, but it is still a long way from being a cheek-by-jowl relationship. This Thayer-Dartmouth experience tends to support C. P. Snow's "Principle of Maximum Purity": that in universities pure science tends to drive out or dominate the applied sciences.

There were, and still are, several on the Thayer Faculty who thought that some sort of undergraduate engineering-based technology major might be attractive to Dartmouth students as having relevance to our technological civilization. This has never materialized though it still remains a peripheral interest of the faculty.

The engineering sciences curriculum was an extremely rigorous, analysis-oriented plan of studies marked by more mathematics, and more advanced treatment of subject matter in mathematics, physics, and chemistry than had been required previously. The number and rigor of the prerequisite and required courses effectively screened out students having only casual interest in engineering. The new arrangement therefore did not have any significant effect on the number of Thayer graduates.

The requirement for entrance to a fifth year of study in the Thayer School was the Bachelor of Arts degree in Engineering Science. But the fifth year studies were designed for two different kinds of students. There were those who were mainly interested in the traditional fields of professional engineering, and there were those who were interested in research in the engineering sciences. While a master's degree had been offered for studies in professional engineering, this was changed to the Bachelor of Engineering degree to be effective with the Class of 1962. On the other hand, the research-oriented student, the "superior student" as the catalog described him, was granted a Master of Science degree.

From an historical point of view, the emphasis on science and the denigration of engineering seemed to be a manifestation of the alternating dominance of science and technology, analysis and synthesis, learning and doing, which may be traced throughout the lifetime of a viable civilization, institution, or individual. However this may be, toward the end of the Kimball Years, after engineering education had learned its new lessons in science and mathematics, it again began to assert more confidently its differences from science. The insertion of the synthesis-oriented sophomore course Introduction to Engineering, late in the Kimball Years, along with the Internship in Engineering courses of Professor Robert Dean, signaled the beginnings of the rise of engineering with its emphasis on macro- or systems-engineering (as opposed to the micro-engineering of the engineering sciences) and increased liaisons with industry for bringing real problems into the curriculum. This was to become one of the dominating characteristics of the succeeding Tribus Years.

Before the Kimball Years, the Thayer School faculty was entirely oriented toward teaching—"the principle of intensive instruction under close supervision." This followed the example of the superb French engineering schools of the nineteenth century. But at the beginning of the Kimball Years, research as distinct from teaching was begun within the Thayer School. Although, beginning with Professor Fletcher in his earliest years, faculty members had engaged in a wide variety of consulting work, from land surveying to bridge design and valuation studies, there is no record of outside funds supporting research in the School until shortly after World War II. The first real research breakthrough was made by Professor of Civil Engineering John Minnich '29 in 1947–48, with a contract for design and testing of a model of an unusual type of highway bridge. The results of his research were used in the design of the prototype which was built across the Monongahela River in Pittsburgh.

During the 1950s, other members of the faculty obtained research grants and contracts which, by the end of the Kimball Years, produced income approaching one-half of the School's total yearly expense. Foremost in this development were Professors Millett Morgan and James Browning: Morgan along the lines of analysis or engineering science, and Browning toward objectives of synthesis or new technology.

Professor Morgan's ionospheric research began to attract international attention in the early fifties. It was to become institutionalized as the Radiophysics Department of the Thayer School and is one of the most, if not the most, successful research projects ever conducted at Dartmouth. Indeed, the early success of Professor Morgan made him an extremely influential force in the development of the engineering sciences at Thayer School and the adoption, later, of the School's MS and PhD programs.

Professor Browning developed into a remarkable teacher-inventor-entrepreneur. His early researches into the nature of combustion were parlayed into new developments of welding and cutting torches and their specialization into metal-coating apparatus. Along with Assistant Professor Merle Thorpe '53, Professor Browning also developed a plasma torch and established the Thermal Dynamics Corporation to manufacture it for a world-wide market.

Attracted to Hanover by the prospect of working for Browning's company and also teaching at Thayer was the energetic and aggressive Professor Robert Dean who became a powerful influence in orienting the Thayer School toward seeking real problems from industry for students to deal with. He saw professional engineering education at Thayer as analogous to medical internship. He demanded high standards of analysis and synthesis from his students and his results were impressive not only to his faculty colleagues but to observers from industry. Dean's educational philosophy and approach were to bloom into Thayer's Industrial Partnership program during the Tribus Years. Professor Dean also became an entrepreneur as founder and president of the Creare Corporation. From the Dean and Browning companies perhaps a dozen different enterprises have been spun off. Both professors parlayed some of their industrial problems into research grants for the School involving Thayer students.

In 1949 Professor George Taylor came to Thayer and set up his Work Simplification Laboratory aimed at developing creative abilities in students via improvements of actual products or processes. Student work done in this lab and submitted in annual national competitions invariably received recognition throughout the Kimball Years for excellence in the form of substantial cash prizes or trophies.

All members of the faculty, shown in the graph on page 88, share credit for the remarkable expansion and transformation of the School during the Kimball Years. As they came to an end, the basic educational system was in equilibrium with the developing trends of the times. Dean Kimball and his faculty had achieved a task which has often been described as more complex and difficult than moving a cemetery.

The exploitation of this remarkable achievement into a complete superstructure of graduate studies, extensive liaisons with industrial concerns, and multi-million-dollar support by foundations was to be achieved by the succeeding dean, Myron Tribus.

CHAPTER 10

The Tribus Years 1961–1969

BY PROFESSOR ALVIN OMAR CONVERSE

On reviewing the record, it appears that the developments at the Thayer School during the Tribus Years can be attributed in large part to three sources. First, in the previous decade, there was an appreciable merging of science and mathematics with engineering, resulting in more attention being paid to the scientific foundations and less attention to the detailed procedures of engineering design. This culminated late in the fifties with the adoption of the Engineering Sciences major.

Second, in 1960 the Trustees of Dartmouth College reviewed the status of the Thayer School and decided that in order to maintain quality and with some hope of increasing enrollment, the School should undergo a transition from associated school to full graduate school status. The associated schools primarily serve the Dartmouth undergraduate by providing the professional or vocational extension of his liberal arts education, whereas a graduate school, in addition, would attract students from other undergraduate schools. Furthermore, a graduate school would grant doctoral degrees and be more involved in research.

Third, there was the educational philosophy of the new dean. Myron Tribus had taught at the University of California at Los Angeles where engineering education was not organized along the lines of the usual departments, and he had developed strong ideas about the importance of doing creative engineering design as well as learning subject matter.

It is important to keep in mind the path that engineering education was taking at the time. The scientific content of engineering and the activity of research had largely replaced design procedure

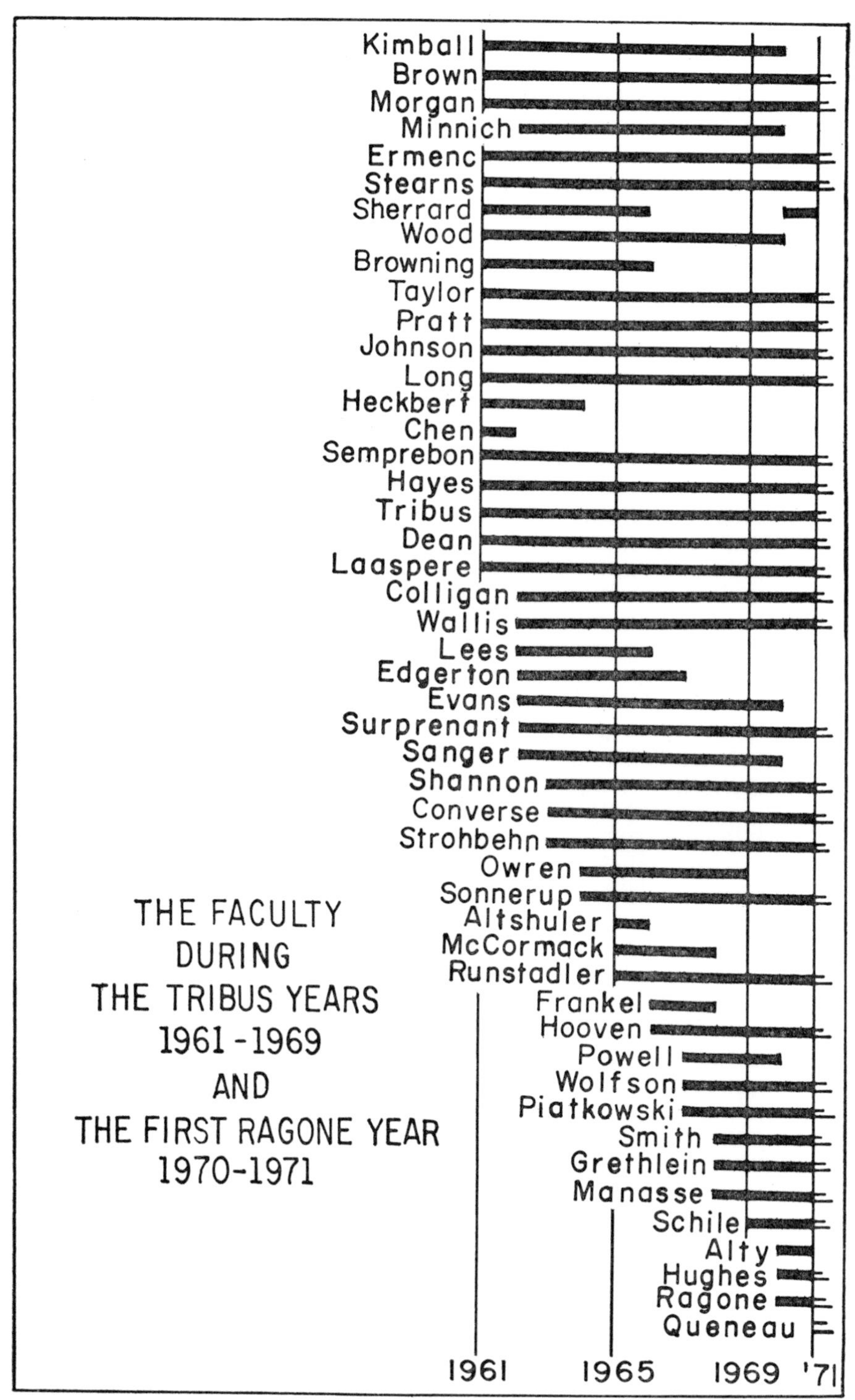
Kimball
Brown
Morgan
Minnich
Ermenc
Stearns
Sherrard
Wood
Browning
Taylor
Pratt
Johnson
Long
Heckbert
Chen
Semprebon
Hayes
Tribus
Dean
Laaspere
Colligan
Wallis
Lees
Edgerton
Evans
Surprenant
Sanger
Shannon
Converse
Strohbehn
Owren
Sonnerup
Altshuler
McCormack
Runstadler
Frankel
Hooven
Powell
Wolfson
Piatkowski
Smith
Grethlein
Manasse
Schile
Alty
Hughes
Ragone
Queneau
THE FACULTY
DURING
THE TRIBUS YEARS
1961-1969
AND
THE FIRST RAGONE YEAR
1970-1971
1961
1965
1969
'71

Figure 8

and the doing of design in engineering schools. In the early 1960s the path was somewhat altered, and Dean Tribus and Thayer School were among the leaders. The alteration was in the direction of design—not back toward proficiency in the skill of routine design procedures, but rather in the direction of innovative or creative design. The computer came along about this time and had the potential of being able to incorporate a great many routine design procedures. Hence, engineering education was free to try a new synthesis of scientific course material with creative design. That synthesis was attempted at the Thayer School to an extent probably not matched anywhere else.

The table below gives some indication of the School's growth during the Tribus Years and the graph on the previous page shows the faculty with whom the growth was accomplished.

Year	*Number of Courses Offered*	*Number of Faculty*	*Number of Staff*	*Annual Budget*	*Total number of Thayer Graduates*
1961	48	18	10	$410,000	
THE TRIBUS YEARS					265
1969	119	34	27	$1,400,000	

Dean Tribus came to Thayer School in the summer of 1961; in November of 1962 he placed a formal proposal for the Master of Engineering and Doctor of Engineering programs before the faculty, and on January 11, 1963, the Trustees of Dartmouth College approved that program. The MSc and PhD programs were delayed somewhat owing to an attempt to form a graduate program in applied sciences that would be interdepartmental. However, that was not realized, and in January 1964 the trustees approved the proposal for a PhD in Engineering Sciences. Also in 1964, the Bachelor of Industrial Administration (BIA) program was discontinued and replaced by a combined Master of Business Administration and Bachelor of Engineering program. During the midsixties, the specialized engineering degree programs were phased out in favor of a unified Bachelor of Engineering degree program, and many new courses were developed in order to fulfill the needs of the graduate programs.

Of the 265 students graduated during the Tribus Years, 66 received master's degrees and 17, doctor's degrees. The School graduated its first PhD, Michael Turner, in 1964 and its first DrE's—Doctors of Engineering—Thomas Black and Andrew Porteous, in 1965.

As shown in the graph and table on pages 25 and 27, outside support of research grew from $186,000 in fiscal year 1961 to $595,000 in fiscal 1969. The latter amount included subcontracts amounting to $139,000 awarded to other colleges and universities from grants and contract funds held by the School's Radiophysics Laboratory. Such subcontracts also accounted for $374,000 of the peak figure of $860,000 in fiscal year 1967. Beginning in the late 1940s, Professor Morgan and his colleagues and assistants—organized as the Radiophysics Laboratory since 1964—have been the largest single source of outside research support. Present members of the Thayer School faculty associated with this laboratory include Professors Laaspere, Strohbehn, and Sonnerup and Research Associates Pratt, Johnson, and Semprebon. Dean Tribus himself was principal investigator on research projects supported by grants amounting to over $100,000 and Associate Dean Colligan directed projects using $70,000 of research funds. Practically all members of the Tribus faculty, in varying degree, engaged in research projects supported by outside funds.

The School was also greatly assisted, during these years, by unrestricted grants from the Sloan Foundation amounting to $2,500,000 and from the Ford Foundation in the amount of $150,000. These grants have been used as expendable funds rather than as a permanent endowment and in 1971 are still contributing to the School's budget.

Since the middle sixties, important support has also been provided by a unique education-industry relationship, based on the concept of shared responsibility, called the Educational Partnership and Thayer Associates Program. This program, initiated by Dean Tribus and carried on, first, by Associate Dean Frankel and, later, by Professor Barnard Smith, is a natural and almost indispensable corollary to the professional programs leading to bachelor's, master's, and doctor's degrees in engineering.

Partners and Associates attend periodic conferences at Thayer

School, receive research reports and other pertinent publications of the School, and have the opportunity to discuss their particular problems with students and faculty members. They also send engineering or management representatives to the School as lecturers or consultants. Frequently, graduate students select thesis topics associated with a company's problems. As Dean Tribus has said, "Industry is the natural source of (creative design) problems. . . . What counts is the educational impact of this experience." The president of a partnership company adds, "The questions raised by young, bright, inquiring minds have a good effect on our staff." In short, the School serves as the laboratory; the company, as the proving ground.

Each partner normally makes an unrestricted contribution of $20,000 per year to the School. The amount of financial support provided by Associates varies. The total income from Partners and Associates between 1966 and 1971 has been approximately $700,000.

The program has led to a higher level of interaction than was at first believed possible and has given students authentic engineering experiences involving professional responsibility and accomplishment. Cooperating companies, in turn, have received a flow of stimulating ideas, some of which have already proven commercially attractive. Thus both the School and the industrial partner or associate have derived financial benefits as well as educational and operating assistance.

It is interesting to note the development of a few courses, particularly by Professors Ermenc and Converse, designed for the nonengineering student. This development has been encouraged by the organizational structure achieved in 1959, that placed engineering faculty in a dual role as members of the Engineering Sciences Department of the College, as well as of the professional School of Engineering. It was a period of relatively rapid growth, and growth that was very innovative.

With strong support from the overseers, the trustees, the Sloan Foundation, and the dean, the faculty made a major change in its way of doing business. The change was very much in keeping with the tradition of a broad liberal arts education coupled with engineering which had been presented in a rather elegant way by Robert Fletcher in 1904:

It is certain that many, heretofore, have turned to a specialty with undue haste, and have found later that it was a mistaken choice, and that they have narrowed their future possibilities; it is also certain that men with the large and more thorough all-around training have been able to adjust themselves to a wider range of emergency and opportunity; while there is force in the argument that in the broader curriculum it is difficult to treat the separate subjects with the necessary thoroughness, it is found in practice that one well trained in the fundamentals seldom fails to fit himself (given a little time) to a special responsibility.

The existing program in Engineering Sciences, which was characterized by rigor and broad coverage, was reviewed and drastically revised. For efficiency, the organization of material has come to be based more on its mathematical structure than on its area of application. There is one exception to the applied science nature of this program and that is the sophomore course Engineering Science 21, Introduction to Engineering. In this course the faculty have attempted to allow the student to experience, or sample, the activity of engineering design. The point emphasized is that this is the essence of engineering practice and that a sophomore student at Dartmouth interested in engineering needs such an experience in order to make a wise choice of major. The course is also intended to give the student a better understanding of the importance of the somewhat abstract studies that follow.

The increased science and mathematics content has aided the development of a unified set of undergraduate courses. A system has many mathematical concepts in common, whether it be electrical, mechanical, or thermal. The distinction is in whether it can be represented by algebraic equations, ordinary differential equations, or partial differential equations. And the undergraduate engineering science core reflects this very strongly. Two courses treat systems represented by algebraic and ordinary differential equations. The courses in Distributed Systems and Fields and in Solid Mechanics treat systems that are represented by partial differential equations. The underlying mathematics of Thermodynamics and Materials Science is largely stochastic. There are reasons other than mathematical for the grouping of these courses, but certainly the mathematical organization is a very strong factor. It is interesting to observe that this resulted in the engineering faculty teaching a set of courses that none of them had taken. Now this occurs quite often within a man's specialty, but there was a sincere attempt here to merge various areas of specialty. As a result, the synthesis and understanding of the undergraduate program have taken a considerable amount of faculty time over these years.

The desire for a more unified presentation of the material also grew out of the interest in creative design. A design problem that starts with the recognition of a human need is very likely to involve several areas of specialization, and it was the view of the faculty that a broad applied science background would allow the student a greater opportunity to participate in the overall synthesis of the device or process being created.

In contrast to the highly structured engineering science undergraduate program, the fifth-year program was then opened up with the student being able to select his courses in any way agreeable to his faculty advisor, so long as it enabled him to indicate abilities described in the 1969–1970 catalog as:

(a) An ability to do analytical and experimental work in engineering or a relevant field. (For example, chemical processing, or biomedical experiment design, or automatic controls, or digital computers might be of interest to the student.) Four or five courses [since changed to "At least three courses . . ."] selected because they support this interest would, if passed successfully, be considered evidence in support of this requirement.
(b) An ability to do creative design. One or more courses in design, methods engineering, or systems engineering, and the successful completion of an individual project will be considered as evidence in support of this requirement.
(c) An ability to analyze the economic aspects of an engineering problem. Successful completion of a course in engineering economy and the analysis of the economic aspects of the individual design project will be considered evidence in support of this requirement.
(d) An ability to analyze and propose a suitable organization for the carrying out of an engineering task.

A generalization of the principle that pure science tends to displace applied science in a university setting is that knowing tends to displace doing at the university. Universities tend to seek truth rather than wisdom and poise. Consider this matter as it is reflected in the motivation of students. There are indeed many people who are excited by learning for learning's sake and building up a storehouse of expertise. To these people, knowing is sufficient unto itself. There is more than a little of that in all of us. However, there is also the desire and the thrill of doing something clever, inventing something new, performing something well. This is the part of education that involves coaching rather than teaching. Students with a large degree of this latter bent are generally attracted into engineering rather than into the pure sciences. It's the doing that is the essence of engineering; it's what engineers build or design, and don't build or design, that really matters. On the other hand, it has to be a very knowledgeable doing. Society can't afford to have the bridge fall down or the reactor explode. The need to see both the forest and the trees is a common problem of the learned professions.

During the sixties, the Thayer School faculty made a concerted effort to resolve this dilemma. That effort took many forms. Fixed equipment laboratories were disassembled and converted to project laboratories in which the design of the experiment, as well as its execution, was the responsibility of the student. Attention was given to the motivational aspects of engineering students. Sociologists and psychiatrists who had studied engineers were invited in to observe and comment on the program here. An education specialist analyzed the program in detail. Professor Sidney Lees showed the lack of correlation of the performance in the engineering design course, ES 21, with mathematics and physics. Both the doing and the knowing were emphasized in the Master of Engineering and Doctor of Engineering programs, as well as in the Master of Science and Doctor of Philosophy programs. For the former two degrees, a student's thesis was required to demonstrate the ability to carry out a creative design, whereas in the latter two the thesis was to demonstrate the ability to generate new knowledge. The fact that the Bachelor of Engineering requirements are written in terms of abilities rather than in terms of the mastery of certain subject matter is another indication of the attempt to incorporate fully the matter of doing into the program. There has been no attempt to incorporate this in admission policies, although early in the sixties there was some inquiry in this direction.

The general tendency of knowing to replace doing in university settings was countered by establishing university degree programs that required evidence of doing.

There has for a long time been a recognition of the degree to which the quality of life is dependent on the nature of our technology. Associated with that realization, there has been a widespread belief, particularly at liberal arts schools, that somehow the presence of an engineering school would contribute to the student's understanding of the importance and the nature of technology. In the early sixties, this aspect of engineering education at Thayer School took a back seat to the development of graduate programs. Toward the end of the decade, however, its importance was more adequately recognized. Today we see new activities in the areas of History of Technology, Community Services, Environmental Studies, and Technology and Public Policy to supplement the longer-established offerings in Legal and Ethical Analysis, Transportation, and Water Resources. One of the difficulties in carrying out this education activity is the fact that engineers generally deal at the level of an individual device or process and not at the level of an industrial complex or technology. There has been a well-established trend, however, through systems analysis and operations research, to generate greater professional interest in this area. This leads to a greater interest in the management of technology. Indeed, the areas of mutual interest between the business school and the engineering school have increased as have the areas of mutual interest between the engineering faculty and the faculty members in the undergraduate college and the medical school.

On the whole, the Tribus Years were a period of growth with innovative and worthwhile programs being implemented.

CHAPTER 11

Sons of Thayer

IT WOULD BE far beyond the capacity of this book to record the many outstanding accomplishments of individual Thayer School alumni. This chapter, therefore, will deal principally with a record of degrees granted and of the organization of the sons of Thayer School, the Dartmouth Society of Engineers.

Biographical information on all the School's alumni was sought every year by Director Fletcher from 1875 to 1918, and increasingly voluminous portions of the Thayer School catalog, or *Annual* as it was called, were devoted to their biographies. From 1920 to 1924, the *Annuals* concentrated on addresses but continued to include some biographical material. After that, the *Annual* became a biennial *Announcement* and contained addresses only. As the alumni body grew, however, the effort and expense involved in obtaining and printing even this limited information, in many cases simply a duplicate of the record from the previous edition, became too great for the School's small staff and the volunteer alumni workers. Beginning in 1936, therefore, the *Announcement* was replaced by a more conventional annual catalog.

The first *Thayer School Register* was published in 1937 as a memorial to Professor Fletcher who had died the year before. It included all the information previously found in the *Thayer School Annuals* and some other features. The second *Thayer School Register*, published in 1948, was dedicated to Dean Garran, who had died three years before, and contained biographical information on all living alumni, class lists, geographical distributions, and other material.

Since 1948, directories of Thayer School alumni have been published periodically. The directories, which have appeared in 1955,

1958, 1964, and 1970, have contained names, addresses, and business affiliations of living alumni.

Of the 1,750 students who have attended Thayer School for at least one year or have completed the School's Engineering Science undergraduate major, 1,265 have been awarded Thayer School degrees. The number of degrees awarded each year from 1873 to 1970 is shown in figure 9, page 107. For the first sixty-eight years, the Civil Engineer degree was the only degree offered. Beginning in 1942, however, other degrees have been granted as shown both in the tabulation below and in figures 9 and 10.

DEGREES

Degrees awarded to Thayer School graduates from 1873 to 1970 are tabulated below and shown graphically on the two following pages.

Degree	*Years*	*Number Awarded*	
CE	1873–1947	522	
BS in CE	1944–47	46	
BCE	1947–48, 1962–68	22	
MS–CE	1947–61	96	
Total Civil Engineering	1873–1968		686
MS–EE	1947–61	82	
BEE	1962–66	20	
Total Electrical Engineering	1947–66		102
MS–ME	1944–61	105	
BME	1948, 1962–66	32	
Total Mechanical Engineering	1944–66		137
MS–TT	1942–61	135	
BIA	1962–64	4	
Total Tuck-Thayer	1942–64		139
Bachelor of Engineering (BE)	1964–70	116	
Master of Engineering (ME)	1964–70	33	
Master of Science (MS)	1961–70	35	
Doctor of Engineering (DrE)	1967–70	9	
Doctor of Philosophy (PhD)	1966–70	8	
Total Undesignated 1961–70			201
Total all Thayer School Degrees 1873–1970			1265

An organization of Thayer alumni was first suggested by Dartmouth President Tucker in the spring of 1902, primarily in order

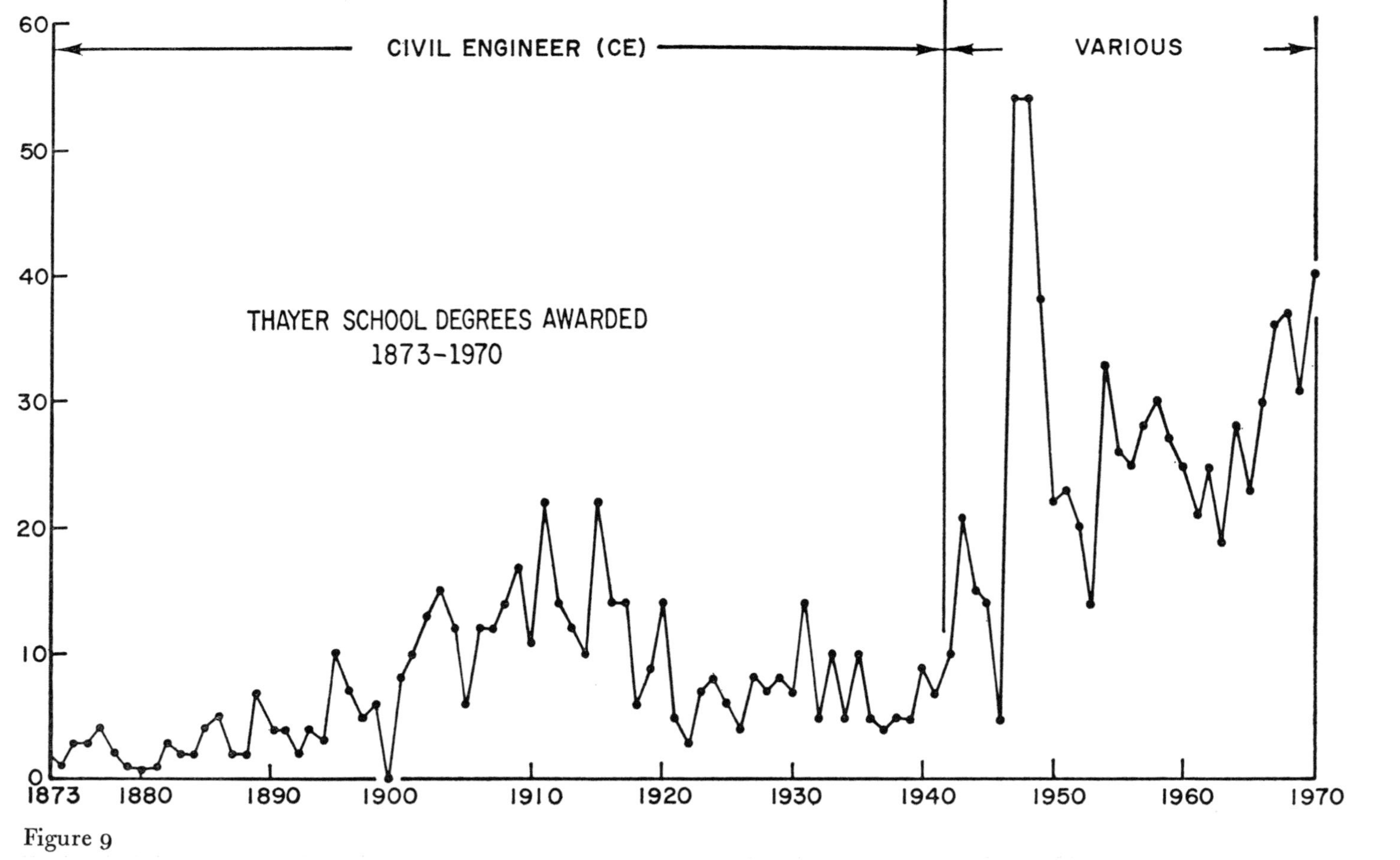
CIVIL ENGINEER (CE)
VARIOUS
THAYER SCHOOL DEGREES AWARDED
1873-1970
60
50
40
30
20
10
0
1873
1880
1890
1900
1910
1920
1930
1940
1950
1960
1970

Figure 9

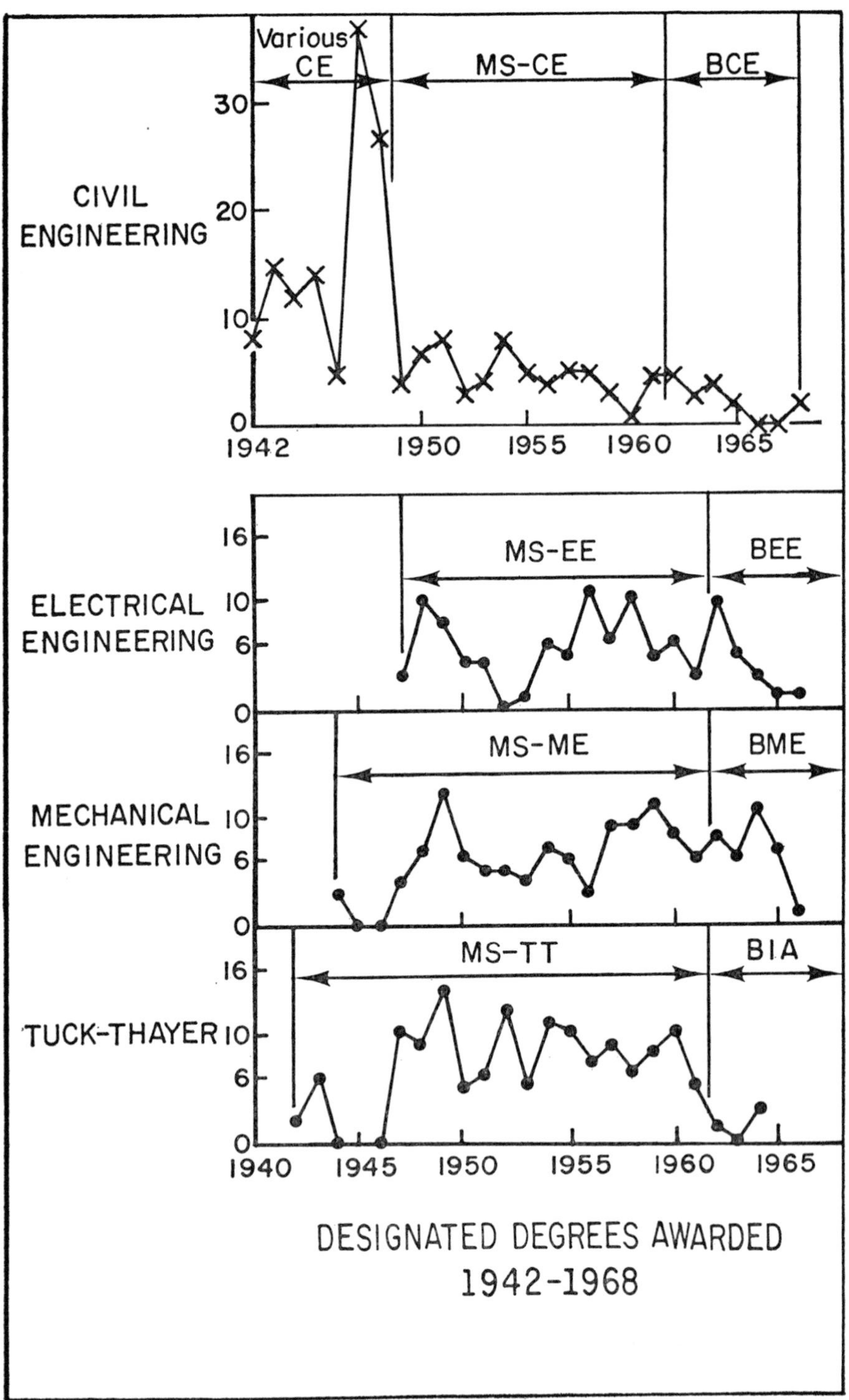
Various CE
MS-CE
BCE
30
20
10
0
CIVIL ENGINEERING
1942
1950
1955
1960
1965
MS-EE
BEE
16
10
6
0
ELECTRICAL ENGINEERING
MS-ME
BME
MECHANICAL ENGINEERING
MS-TT
BIA
TUCK-THAYER
1940
1945
1950
1955
1960
1965
DESIGNATED DEGREES AWARDED
1942-1968

Figure 10

to stimulate an interest in procuring financial backing for the School. A meeting was held in New York City on June 12 of that year with an attendance of twenty-four including President Tucker, Professor Fletcher, and two members of the Board of Overseers. This was to prove a momentous event for it led to the formation of the Thayer Society of Engineers which, since 1945 under the name of the Dartmouth Society of Engineers, has provided vital assistance to the School both financially and by many supportive activities.

The statement of purpose in the original constitution of the Society was simply "to further the interests of the Thayer School of Civil Engineering; to promote social intercourse among its members, and to keep them informed as concerns the work and needs of said school." How well the Society had accomplished its purposes was testified to by Dean Garran who wrote, in 1945, "Much of the credit for the enviable position of the Thayer School among the engineering schools of the country is due to her alumni; both because of the high standard of professional accomplishment attained by them individually and because of their collective loyalty to the School, financially and spiritually, expressed through the medium of the Thayer Society of Engineers of Dartmouth College. I believe it is literally true that, lacking the extraordinary support organized among its members by the Thayer Society, the Thayer School might now be a subject of historic interest only."

The alumni who have led the Society over the years are listed in Appendix C. It is appropriate to enter here the extent of financial support developed by the Society. This has taken several forms: the Dartmouth Society of Engineers Endowment Fund amounting in 1970 to $7,100, the income from which is available for current expenses of the School; the Dartmouth Society of Engineers Loan Fund amounting in 1969 to $2,700 and available to "needy and worthy students"; and the annual gifts for current operating expenses of the School. The gifts for current expenses grew from modest beginnings in 1905 to a high of $6,750 in 1925 and totaled over $85,000 during the critical period between 1905 and 1943.

In 1925, the Society organized the Robert Fletcher Fund along the lines of the College's Alumni Fund, as a vehicle for collecting alumni contributions. The fund's effectiveness is demonstrated by the increase in the Society's contribution to the School from $1,000 in 1924 to $6,750 in 1925. Contributions held up well for a few years but soon began to reflect the economic depression of the thirties which hit engineers especially hard. By 1937, despite heroic efforts to meet more optimistic quotas, the fund grossed only $2,200. Also, by this time it became recognized both by workers for the Fletcher Fund and by those working for the College's Alumni Fund that the solicitations were competitive and that more was probably lost in good will than was gained in dollars. It was therefore agreed that, beginning in 1938, the Thayer Society of Engineers would urge its members to increase their contributions to the Alumni Fund in lieu of contributing to the separate funds. The College agreed, on its part, to allocate a portion of Alumni Fund receipts to Thayer School income. The allocations increased from $2,400 in 1938 to $3,900 in 1943 and have been included in the $85,000 total noted above.

The original purpose of the Society has been somewhat broadened as reflected in the constitution adopted in 1957 which states its objectives to be threefold:

> To bring together men of Dartmouth interested in engineering . . . for better acquaintance, fellowship and mutual helpfulness. . . .
>
> To sponsor a Student Chapter . . . and [to make it] an active and purposeful student organization [by] advising on current engineering opportunities, participating in lectures . . . and [performing] other services that help to cement the relations between the undergraduate society and the parent organization.
>
> To promote interchange of ideas between graduates and faculty and to strengthen the tie between its members and Thayer School, to the end that the interests, influences, and efficiency of Dartmouth College may be advanced through its Associated School of Engineering.

In furtherance of these objectives, the Society officers have taken a keen interest in the welfare of the School. Meetings are held annually both in New York City and in Boston. The ten-man Executive Committee also meets annually in Hanover. This meeting includes a joint session with the Board of Overseers, social and business get-togethers with the faculty, and a banquet for the graduating class.

In 1928, the Society undertook to stimulate student interest in engineering projects by offering a prize of fifty dollars to the Thayer

School student writing the best report on an engineering subject. The prize has been awarded annually since it was established. Since 1957, awards have been authorized for more than one student whenever papers on diverse subjects have been judged by the faculty to be of equal merit. A complete list of recipients and the titles of the award-winning papers will be found in Appendix D.

In 1949 the Charles F. and Ruth D. Goodrich Prize was established to be awarded annually "to the second-year Thayer School or Tuck-Thayer student who has achieved the highest all-around record." The late Dr. Goodrich '06 was president of the Dartmouth Society of Engineers from 1923 to 1929 and served on the Board of Overseers from 1941 to 1956. Dartmouth's honorary Doctor of Engineering degree was bestowed on him by President Hopkins in 1939. In establishing the prize, the Goodrichs specified that "in determining the recipient . . . scholastic accomplishment, particularly in second-year work, [should be] a major consideration." The income of the prize fund is available to the recipient for the purchase of engineering books of his choosing. A list of recipients will be found in Appendix E.

Epilogue

THE TRIBUS YEARS came to an end in mid-March 1969 when Dean Tribus accepted appointment as Assistant Secretary of Commerce for Science and Technology and moved immediately to that post in Washington, D.C. Associate Dean George A. Colligan was named acting dean but in June indicated his wish to relinquish these duties and resume his previous activities as Professor and Associate Dean. He agreed, however, to remain as acting dean until September when Dartmouth's Associate Provost William P. Davis agreed to serve as acting dean on a part-time basis until a new appointment could be made to fill the vacant deanship.

Davis was a popular choice with the Thayer School faculty. Having formerly been Professor of Physics, he was well known and well liked by his new colleagues. Although continuing to carry a heavy load of administrative work for the College, he conscientiously and successfully conducted what could only be a holding operation in the Thayer School dean's office until July 1970 when Dr. David Vincent Ragone became the seventh in the School's hundred-year succession of deans. On leaving his temporary Thayer School assignment, Dr. Davis was named by President Kemeny to the newly created post of Budget Officer.

Under Acting Dean Davis, all of the normal activities of the School—instruction, research, and industrial cooperation—continued without interruption or disruption throughout the 1969–70 academic year. In addition, substantial progress was made in developing joint activities with both the Medical School and the Tuck School.

Two other sources of strength during the transition year were Thayer School's Executive Officer Desmond E. Canavan and the Board of Overseers. Colonel Canavan furnished the invaluable daily support which gave the acting dean the information and guidance which only years of experience could provide. The overseers, on their part, made efforts far beyond the usual call of Board duty to assure that the momentum which had been generated during the Tribus Years should not be lost.

Although 1969–70 can only be recorded as a year of transition, Acting Dean Davis performed an invaluable service in keeping the School on an even keel. Thanks to his calm, cheerful, and unassuming manner and his constant attention to the welfare of the School, it was possible for Dean Ragone to take up very nearly where Dean Tribus had left off. Thayer School and Dartmouth owe him a debt of gratitude.

Dean David Vincent Ragone will lead the School from its first century into its second. He brings to his new position a background of education and experience which is in the tradition of Thayer School's emphasis on breadth with depth. After receiving bachelor's, master's, and doctor's degrees in metallurgical engineering in successive years from MIT, he taught in the Department of Chemical and Metallurgical Engineering at the University of Michigan for several years. During the following five years, he was Chairman of the Metallurgy Department of the General Atomic Division of General Dynamics. He was then appointed ALCOA Professor of Metallurgy at Carnegie-Mellon University. He served as Associate Dean of Carnegie's School of Urban and Public Affairs during the year preceding his appointment to Thayer School.

While occupied in these positions, he has compiled a list of over thirty publications, has served as consultant to several corporations, has held directorships in three companies, and has been appointed to many government and professional committees. The breadth of his many interests is suggested by the committee assignments which have included the U. S. Department of Commerce's Technical Advisory Board and its panels on housing technology, automotive fuels, power systems, and air pollution; a Presidential panel on unconventional engines; and committees on such diverse subjects as electric cars, education, and nuclear metallurgy.

Still in his first year at Thayer School, he has taken positions on the present program and proposed certain new emphases and directions for the future. He subscribes without reservation to the School's long tradition of engineering education based on, and interacting with, the liberal arts and basic sciences. He recognizes that the Thayer School–Engineering Science Department relationship with the undergraduate College provides a unique opportunity for extensive interdisciplinary attention to many of today's most urgent societal needs. He supports the views of members of his faculty who believe that the School has an obligation to offer instruction in technology to Dartmouth undergraduates whose programs are primarily in the humanities and social sciences. He is also determined that, based on the undergraduate engineering sciences major, the parallel stems of science and engineering in Thayer School's graduate instructional program will work together toward the School's goals and objectives. "One of the primary goals in the science stem," Dean Ragone says, "will be concentration in a limited number of basic areas in which faculty strength presently exists."

"The professional program," he continues, "will have two areas of concentration: Engineering Design, and Technology and Public Policy. These two areas, will, of course, interact with each other and will continue to stress problem solving as in the present physical design courses related to products and processes. However, new emphasis will be placed on problems having their genesis in the public sector because the Dartmouth–Thayer School environment is ideally suited to the interdisciplinary approach which is vital to their solution."

Areas of interest in this new program on Technology and Public Policy will be determined by present and foreseeable future social needs and may include such subjects as air and water quality, solid waste management, radioactivity, thermal effects, energy management, community services such as police, fire, snow removal, and medical care, education, and national technology policy. It is clear that the Dartmouth-Thayer approach to these problems can and must be through close cooperation among various departments of the College and special groups such as the Public Affairs Center and all three of the associated schools.

And so, Thayer School closes out its first century and looks to the needs of society and to the resources of all of Dartmouth to chart its course into its second hundred years.

Appendixes

APPENDIX A

Board of Overseers

THE FOLLOWING PERSONS have served on the Board of Overseers, beginning with the original appointments of General Thayer in 1867. Class numerals without designation indicate Thayer School alumni. Dartmouth alumni who are not Thayer alumni are designated by D. Honorary Dartmouth degrees, indicated by h, are shown only for those who did not attend Dartmouth as undergraduates. The President of Dartmouth College was Chairman of the Board of Overseers ex officio from 1867 to 1957. The Provost of Dartmouth College was Board Chairman ex officio from 1957 to 1967. Since 1967, the President has appointed the Chairman of the Board from its membership.

Bar charts showing concurrence of terms will be found on pages 20 and 21.

ASA D. SMITH D '30, 1867–1877
President of Dartmouth College

DENNIS H. MAHAN, 1867–1871
Professor of Engineering, United States Military Academy

OLIVER P. HUBBARD D '73h, 1867–1895
Hall Professor of Mineralogy and Geology and Professor of Chemistry and Pharmacy, Dartmouth College

GEORGE L. ANDREWS D '73h, 1867–1899
Brevet Major-General, United States Army, United States Marshal for Massachusetts, and Professor of French, United States Military Academy

JOHN C. PALFREY D '73h, 1867–1906
General, United States Army, and Manufacturer

PETER S. MICHIE D '73h, 1871–1901
Professor of Natural and Experimental Philosophy, United States Military Academy

SAMUEL C. BARTLETT D '36, 1877–1892
President of Dartmouth College

WILLIAM J. TUCKER D '61, 1892–1909
President of Dartmouth College

Henry L. Abbot, 1895–1918
Brigadier General, United States Army

Jonathan P. Snow '75, 1899–1925
Chief Engineer, Boston and Maine Railroad, and Consulting Engineer

Gustav J. Fiebeger, 1901–1924
Retired Colonel, United States Army

Otis E. Hovey '89, 1907–1941
Assistant Chief Engineer, American Bridge Company, and Consulting Engineer

Ernest F. Nichols D '03h, 1909–1916
President of Dartmouth College

Ernest M. Hopkins D '01, 1916–1945
President of Dartmouth College

Robert Fletcher D '71h, 1918–1925, Clerk 1925–1936*
Director Emeritus, Thayer School of Civil Engineering

Arthur C. Tozzer '03, 1924–1942
Vice President, Turner Construction Company

Edwin J. Morrison '93, 1925–1936
President and Director, Hastings Pavement Company

Arthur W. French '92, 1925–1939
Professor of Civil Engineering, Worcester Polytechnic Institute, and Consulting Engineer

Charles R. Main '08, 1936–1942
Treasurer, Charles T. Main, Inc.

Luther S. Oakes '00, 1940–1953
Chairman of the Board, Winston Brothers Company, Contractors

Charles F. Goodrich '06, 1941–1956
Chief Engineer, American Bridge Company

Frank E. Cudworth '02, 1943–1956
Chief Engineer, Walsh-Kaiser Company, Shipbuilding Division, and Construction Engineer

Richard E. Pritchard '15, 1945–1957
Chairman of the Board, The Stanley Works

John S. Dickey D '29, 1945–1970
President of Dartmouth College

Henry N. Muller, Jr. D '35, 1953–1961
Vice President and Chief Engineer, Canadian Westinghouse Company, Ltd.

J. Hartness Beardsley D '37, 1956–1963
President and General Manager, Twin Falls Power Corporation, Ltd.

Herbert F. Darling '27, 1956–1964
President, Herbert F. Darling Company, General Contractors

* As Clerk, Dr. Fletcher was de facto but not officially a member of the Board.

Thomas B. Curtis D '32, 1957–1958
Representative, United States Congress, and Trustee of Dartmouth College

Frederick A. Davidson '15, 1957–1958
President, Refined Syrups and Sugars, Inc.

Donald H. Morrison, D '47h, 1957–1959, Chairman
Provost of Dartmouth College

Jess H. Davis, 1957–1964
President, Stevens Institute of Technology

John C. Woodhouse D '21, 1957–1968
Director, Reactor Materials and Explosives Department, Atomic Energy Division, E. I. Du Pont de Nemours & Company, and Trustee of Dartmouth College.

Gordon S. Brown D '64h, 1957–1965, 1970–
Dean of Engineering and Dugald C. Jackson Professor of Electrical Engineering, Massachusetts Institute of Technology

Ralph W. Hunter D '31, 1958–1961
Physician, Mary Hitchcock Memorial Hospital and Clinic, and Trustee of Dartmouth College

E. Shaw Cole '31, 1958–1966
President, Pitometer Associates, Consulting Engineers

John W. Masland D '46h, 1959–1967, Chairman
Provost of Dartmouth College

Charles C. Leader, 1961–1969
Manager, Administrative Consulting Engineering Services, General Electric Company

Henry J. McCarthy D '31, 1961–1970
President, Trimac Engineering, Inc.

James H. Wakelin, Jr. D '32, 1963–1971, Chairman 1967–1970
Chief Scientist, Ryan Aeronautical Company, and Assistant Secretary of Commerce for Science and Technology

David M. Lilly D '39, 1964– , Chairman 1970–
Chairman of the Board, Toro Manufacturing Company

Robert T. Barr '42, 1964–
Chairman of the Board, Barr & Barr, Inc., Contractors

John G. Truxal D '45, 1965–1969
Dean of Engineering, Provost, and Vice President, Polytechnic Institute of Brooklyn

Henry C. Beck, Jr. '39, 1966–
President, Henry C. Beck, Inc., Contractors

Leonard M. Rieser, Jr. D '44, 1967–
Provost of Dartmouth College

John D. Dodd D '22, 1968–
Retired Vice President, New York Bell Telephone Company, and Trustee of Dartmouth College

John B. Cook D '29, 1969–
Chairman and Director, Whitney Blake Company

Donald N. Frey, 1969–
President, General Cable Corporation, and Chairman of the Board of Bell and Howell Corporation

John G. Kemeny D '56h, 1970–
President of Dartmouth College

William F. May, 1970–
Executive Committee Member and Director, American Can Company

John E. Schlachtenhaufen '63, 1970–
Assistant Production Manager, Communication Products Division, Xerox Corporation

David V. Ragone, 1970–
Dean of Thayer School

APPENDIX B

Faculty

THE FOLLOWING LIST contains the names of all faculty members from 1871 to 1971 who have held a full-time or adjunct appointment of the rank of Instructor, Research Assistant, or higher. Not included, with a few exceptions, are those who have taught one or more courses in Thayer School while holding a regular appointment either on the Dartmouth faculty or on the faculty of another college or university. Also not included are those who have held an appointment only as Assistant, Teaching Fellow, Graduate Assistant in Research, Post-doctoral Fellow, or Lecturer. Therefore, a few names which have been included in previous faculty lists have been omitted here.

Listing is chronological according to the year of first appointment. When two or more were first appointed in the same year, length of tenure determines order of listing.

Recipients of Thayer School's Civil Engineer degree, most of whom also hold a Dartmouth Bachelor's degree, are simply designated by a class numeral. Other Dartmouth or Thayer School degrees are shown without designation of the institution awarding the degree. All Dartmouth AM degrees shown are, with a single exception, honorary.

ROBERT FLETCHER, USMA; AM, PhD, DSc; Thayer Professor of Civil Engineering 1871–1918; Director 1892–1918; Emeritus 1918–36.

CHARLES H. PETTEE, '76; AM; Instructor in Civil Engineering 1876–77.

JONATHAN P. SNOW, '75; Instructor in Civil Engineering 1877–78.

JOHN A. WORTHEN, '77; Instructor in Civil Engineering 1880–81.

JOHN W. RECORD, '77; Instructor in Civil Engineering 1881–82.

HIRAM A. HITCHCOCK, '81; Instructor in Civil Engineering 1883–87; Associate Professor 1887–95.

JOHN V. HAZEN, '76, AM; Woodman Professor of Civil Engineering and Graphics on the Chandler Foundation 1891–1919.

ARTHUR W. FRENCH, '92; Assistant Professor of Civil Engineering 1895–97; Associate Professor 1897–98.

John L. Mann, '98; Assistant Professor of Civil Engineering 1899–1903; Associate Professor 1903–05.

Charles A. Holden, '01; Instructor in Civil Engineering 1900–04; Assistant Professor 1904–05; Associate Professor 1905–08; Professor 1908–25, 1934–35; Director 1918–25; Emeritus 1935.

Frank E. Austin, BS, EE; Instructor in Electrical Engineering 1902–08; Professor 1908–21.

Morton O. Withey, '05; Instructor in Civil Engineering 1905–06.

Charles H. Hoyt, '01; Instructor in Civil Engineering 1907–08.

Frederick W. Welch, '08; Instructor in Civil Engineering 1908–09.

Raymond R. Marsden, '09; Instructor in Civil Engineering 1909–10; Professor 1919–33; Dean 1925–33.

Sydney L. Ruggles, '09; Instructor in Civil Engineering 1910–20.

Allen P. Richmond, Jr., '15; Assistant Professor of Civil Engineering 1919–29.

Harold J. Lockwood, Lafayette EE, MS; Assistant Professor of Electrical Engineering 1919–21; Professor 1921–34.

Frank W. Garran, Norwich BS in CE; MIT SM; Assistant Professor of Civil Engineering 1929–33; Professor and Dean 1933–45.

William P. Kimball, '29, AM; Assistant 1929–30; Instructor in Civil Engineering 1933–35; Assistant Professor 1935–39; Professor 1939–66; Assistant Dean 1941–45; Dean 1945–61; Adjunct Professor 1966–70; Emeritus, 1970– .

Edgar J. Tuite, RPI EE; Instructor in Power Engineering 1932–33.

Clifford P. Kittredge, MIT SB; Munich DrIng; Instructor in Power Engineering 1933–34.

James R. Hicks, Georgia Institute of Technology BS in ME; Assistant Professor of Power Engineering 1935–37.

Hill R. Nettles, U. of South Carolina CE; Lehigh MS; Instructor in Civil Engineering 1936–37.

Arthur N. Daniels, U. S. Naval Academy BS; Harvard MS in ME; Instructor of Power Engineering 1937–40; Assistant Professor 1940–41.

Edward S. Brown, '35; Harvard SM; Instructor in Civil Engineering 1937–40; Assistant Professor 1940–45; Professor 1945– .

Kenneth K. Edgar, Ohio State U. BS in CE, MS in IE; Assistant Professor of Industrial Engineering 1941–42.

Harald Schutz, Technische Hochshule DrTechSci; Instructor in Power Engineering 1941–42; Assistant Professor 1942–44.

Millett G. Morgan, Cornell AB, MS in Engg; Stanford Engr., PhD; AM; Instructor in Power Engineering 1941–44; Assistant

Professor of Electrical Engineering 1947–53; Assistant Dean 1947–50; Director of Research 1950–63; Professor 1953– ; Sydney E. Junkins Professor of Engineering 1971– ; Director of Radiophysics Laboratory 1964– .

CHARLES Y. HITCHCOCK, JR., '39; Instructor in Civil Engineering 1942.

FREDERICK J. KNIGHTS, U. of Nebraska BS in EE; Northwestern MBA; Assistant Professor of Industrial Engineering 1942–44.

JOHN H. MINNICH, '29, AM; Assistant Professor of Civil Engineering 1942–45; Professor 1945–56; Visiting Professor 1962–64; Adjunct Professor 1964–70; Emeritus 1970– .

JOSEPH J. ERMENC, U. of Wisconsin BS; U. of Michigan MS; AM; Assistant Professor of Mechanical Engineering 1942–45; Professor 1945–66; Professor of Engineering 1966– .

WILLIAM H. KIMBALL, Consulting Engineer; Special Instructor in Civil Engineering 1943.

PAUL S. STAPLES, BS; Instructor in Engineering 1943–44.

MALCOLM D. CORNER, BS; Instructor in Engineering 1943–44.

LEROY F. BRIGGS, BS; Instructor in Engineering 1943–44.

JAMES P. POOLE, U. of Maine BS; Harvard AM, PhD; Professor of Botany; Instructor in Surveying and Graphics 1943–45.

ROBERT P. TRAINOR, Lowell Technological Institute; Instructor in Mechanical Engineering 1944.

NATHAN H. RICH, U. of Maine BS in ME; Instructor in Mechanical Engineering 1944–45.

NORMAN E. WILSON, Cornell EE; Assistant Professor of Electrical Engineering 1944–45.

FRANCIS R. DRURY, '38; Assistant Professor of Civil Engineering 1944–46.

REXFORD G. MOULTON, Syracuse BSME, BSAE; Assistant Professor of Mechanical Engineering 1944–50.

JOHN M. HIRST, '39; Northwestern MS; Instructor in Electrical Engineering 1944–45; Assistant Professor 1945–55.

S. RUSSELL STEARNS, '38; Purdue MS; Instructor in Civil Engineering 1945; Assistant Professor 1945–53; Professor 1953– .

EDWARD J. BUTLER, Rutgers BSEE; Assistant Professor of Engineering and Management 1946–47.

WILLIAM J. ECKEL, New York U. BEE; Lafayette MS; Instructor in Electrical Engineering 1946–49.

EDWIN A. SHERRARD, McGill BSc; AM; Assistant Professor of Mechanical Engineering 1946–52; Professor 1952–65; Emeritus 1966– ; Adjunct Professor 1971– .

J. ALBERT WOOD, JR., Cornell EE, PhD; AM; U. of Rochester MSc; Assistant Professor of Electrical Engineering 1946–48; Professor 1948–70; Emeritus 1970– .

Edmund J. Byrkit, MS-CE '47; Instructor in Civil Engineering 1947–48.

Byron S. Dague, U. S. Naval Academy BS; Columbia MS; Assistant Professor of Engineering and Management 1948–49.

Robert E. Keane, MS-CE '48; Instructor in Civil Engineering 1948–49.

John P. Hatch, Duke BSME; New York U. MME; Instructor in Mechanical Engineering 1949–52; Assistant Professor 1952–53.

James A. Browning, AB; Stanford MS; AM; Instructor in Mechanical Engineering 1949–52; Assistant Professor 1952–57; Associate Professor 1957–60; Professor 1960–62; Adjunct Professor 1962–66.

George A. Taylor, New York U. BS, MS; AM; Assistant Professor of Engineering and Management 1949–1951; Professor 1951– .

Peter S. Dow, '11, Professor of Engineering Drawing 1950–52, Emeritus 1952– .

Donald L. Pyke, Purdue BS, MS; Instructor in Applied Mechanics 1950–51; Assistant Professor 1951–55; Assistant to the Dean 1950–53; Acting Dean 1953–54; Assistant Dean 1954–55.

Blanchard Pratt, MS-EE '51; Research Assistant 1950–51; Research Associate 1951– .

W. Cutting Johnson, AB, AM; Research Assistant 1951–54; Research Associate 1954– .

William B. Conway, MS-CE '54; Teaching Fellow in Engineering 1952–54; Instructor in Civil Engineering 1954–55.

Merle L. Thorpe, MS-ME '53; Research Assistant 1952–53; Instructor in Mechanical Engineering 1956–58; Assistant Professor 1958–60; Assistant to the Dean 1956–57.

Kenneth A. LeClair, U. of Massachusetts BS, MS; Instructor in Civil Engineering 1952–54; Assistant Professor 1954–58.

Robert M. Jodrey, Worcester Polytechnic Institute BS; Instructor in Mechanical Engineering 1953–54.

Charles Kingsley, Jr., MIT SB, SM; Visiting Professor of Electrical Engineering 1953–55.

Huntington W. Curtis, William and Mary BS; U. of New Hampshire MS; State U. of Iowa PhD; Assistant Professor of Electrical Engineering 1953–59.

Chi-Neng Shen, National Tsing Hua U. BSc; U. of Minnesota MSc, PhD; Assistant Professor of Mechanical Engineering 1954–58.

Carl F. Long, MIT SB, SM; Yale DrEng; Instructor in Civil Engineering 1954–56; Assistant Professor 1957–64; Associate Professor of Engineering 1964–70; Professor 1970– .

Raymond F. Mosher, MIT SB, SM; Visiting Professor of Electrical Engineering 1955–58.

Charles C. Reynolds, MIT SB, SM; Assistant Professor of Mechanical Engineering and Assistant Dean 1957–60.

Albert I. Heckbert, Tufts BS; MIT SM; RPI PhD; Assistant Professor of Electrical Engineering 1957–59; Associate Professor 1959–63.

Bertram Wellman, Harvard BS; MIT MS; Visiting Assistant Professor of Electrical Engineering 1958–60.

Tien Y. Chen, St. John's U. BA; Polytechnic Institute of Brooklyn MCE; U. of Illinois PhD; Associate Professor of Civil Engineering 1958–62.

Samuel A. Werner, MS-ES '61; Teaching Fellow 1959–60; Instructor in Engineering Science 1960–61.

Louis C. Semprebon, UCLA AB; MS-EE '61; Research Assistant 1960–68; Research Associate 1968– .

Miles V. Hayes, Yale AB; MIT SB; Harvard MA, PhD; Visiting Associate Professor of Engineering 1960–62; Associate Professor 1962–64; Professor 1970.

Myron Tribus, U. of California, Berkeley BS; UCLA PhD; AM; Professor of Engineering 1961–70; Dean 1961–69; Adjunct Professor, 1971– .

Robert C. Dean, Jr., MIT SB, SM, ScD; Visiting Associate Professor of Engineering 1961–62; Associate Professor 1962–66; Professor 1966– .

Thomas Laaspere, U. of Vermont BSEE; Cornell MS, PhD; Assistant Professor of Engineering 1961–64; Associate Professor 1964–70; Professor 1970– .

George A. Colligan, RPI BMetE; U. of Michigan MSE, PhD; AM; Associate Professor of Engineering 1962–65; Professor 1965– ; Associate Dean 1967– ; Acting Dean 1969.

Graham B. Wallis, Cambridge, England BA, MA, PhD; MIT SM; Assistant Professor of Engineering 1962–66; Associate Professor 1966– .

Sidney Lees, CCNY BS; MIT SM, ScD; Professor of Engineering 1962–66.

Robert H. Edgerton, U. of Connecticut BS, MS; Cornell PhD; Assistant Professor of Engineering 1962–67.

Robert B. Evans, UCLA BS, MS; Dartmouth PhD; Research Associate 1962–70.

Victor A. Surprenant, U. of Connecticut AB; Research Assistant 1962–69; Research Associate 1970– .

Frederick J. Sanger, U. of London BSc; MSc; Imperial College of Science & Technology, Dip; Visiting Professor of Engineering 1962–63; Adjunct Professor 1963–70.

PAUL T. SHANNON, Illinois Institute of Technology BS, PhD; Associate Professor of Engineering 1963–67; Professor 1967– .

ALVIN O. CONVERSE, Lehigh BS; U. of Delaware MChE, PhD; Associate Professor of Engineering 1963–70; Professor 1970– .

JOHN W. STROHBEHN, Stanford BS, MS, PhD; Assistant Professor of Engineering 1963–68; Associate Professor 1968– .

LEIF OWREN, U. of Oslo BS, MS; Cornell PhD; AM; Professor of Engineering 1964–69.

BENGT U. O. SONNERUP, Chalmers Institute of Technology, Gothenburg, Sweden BME; Cornell MAeroE, PhD; Associate Professor of Engineering 1964–69; Professor 1970– .

THOMAS L. ALTSHULER, U. of California, Berkeley BS; Columbia MS; Oxford, England PhD; Associate Professor of Engineering 1965–66.

PERCIVAL D. MCCORMACK, Trinity College, Dublin BS, MSc, MA; Dublin Institute for Advanced Studies PhD; Professor of Engineering 1965–68.

PETER W. RUNSTADLER, JR., Stanford MA, MS, PhD; Assistant Professor of Engineering 1965–68; Adjunct Professor 1968– .

JACOB P. FRANKEL, U. of California, Berkeley BS, MS; UCLA PhD; Professor of Engineering 1966–68; Associate Dean 1967–68.

FREDERICK J. HOOVEN, MIT BS; Adjunct Professor of Engineering 1966– .

GRAHAM L. F. POWELL, U. of New South Wales, Australia BS; U. of Queensland MS, PhD; Research Associate 1967–70.

ROBERT G. WOLFSON, MIT BS; Northwestern MS, PhD; Associate Professor of Engineering 1967– .

THOMAS F. PIATKOWSKI, U. of Michigan BSE, MSE, PhD; Assistant Professor of Engineering 1967–69; Associate Professor 1969– .

BARNARD E. SMITH, U. of Minnesota BSME; Stanford PhD; Professor of Engineering 1968– .

HANS E. GRETHLEIN, Drexel BS in ChE; Princeton PhD; Associate Professor of Engineering 1968– .

FRED K. MANASSE, CCNY BEE; Princeton MA, PhD; Associate Professor of Engineering 1968– .

RICHARD D. SCHILE, RPI BA, MS, PhD; Associate Professor of Engineering 1969– .

CHRISTOPHER J. N. ALTY, Queen's College, Cambridge, England BA, Sc Tripos, PhD; Visiting Associate Professor 1970–71.

JAMES M. HUGHES, BE '66; Research Assistant 1970–71.

DAVID V. RAGONE, MIT SB, SM, ScD; Professor of Engineering and Dean 1970– .

PAUL E. QUENEAU, Columbia BA, BS, EM; Adjunct Professor of Engineering 1971– .

STAFF

It is not feasible to list all the efficient and loyal people who have served the Thayer School over the years without faculty rank. However, even at the risk of unintentional slight, the following staff members are noted because they performed individual services for *every* student and member of the faculty during the years of their tenure:

Barbara (Beetle) Brown, Secretary and Librarian 1933–37.
Mildred Smith, Secretary 1937–39.
Ruth Bristol, Secretary and Librarian 1939–43.
Della Hall, Secretary 1943–47.
Abbie Metcalf, Librarian 1943–69.
Larry Goldthwaite, Technician 1948–63.
Stacia (Kebalka) Ballou, Secretary 1951–60.
Ellen Gellerman, Secretary 1953–68.
Marion Morhouse, Secretary and Registrar 1957– .
Des Canavan, Executive Officer 1962– , Assistant Dean 1971– .
Ross Hunter, Technician 1963–69.

APPENDIX C

Dartmouth Society of Engineers Officers, 1904–1971

THE 112 alumni of the Thayer School of Dartmouth College who have served as officers, members of the Advisory Board, or members of the Executive Committee of the Dartmouth Society of Engineers—named the Thayer Society of Engineers until 1945—are listed below in the chronological order of their first appointments. The Advisory Board was terminated in 1934. The office of vice president was established in 1949. From 1904 to 1951 the annual meeting of the Society was held in January and officer's terms were for calendar years. Since then, the annual meetings have been held in October and officers' terms have begun at that time.

Name and Class	*President*	*Treasurer*	*Secretary*	*Advisory Board*	*Executive Committee*
John J. Hopper '85	1904–09				1904–09
George P. Bard '89		1904–08		1914–16, 1919–21	1904–08
Charles H. Nichols '88	1912–13		1904–09		1904–09, 1912–13
Edgar R. Cate '01					1904–05
John A. McNicol '82				1910–12	1904–05
Robert Fletcher, USMA '68				1904–34	
Arthur W. French '92				1904–10, 1911–13, 1915–17, 1919–21, 1923–25	

Name and Class	*President*	*Treasurer*	*Secretary*	*Advisory Board*	*Executive Committee*
Otis E. Hovey '89		1908–11		1904–06	1906–12, 1917–24
George H. Hutchinson '84				1904–08	
Henry M. Paul '75				1904–05, 1922–24	
William H. Pratt '74				1904–05, 1912–14	
Hiram N. Savage '90				1904–10, 1917–19	
Amasa B. Clark '89	1909–10, 1919–22				1905–12, 1919–21
Edwin J. Morrison '93	1915–19				1905–06, 1907–10, 1915–19, 1922–26
John V. Hazen '76				1905–11	
Jonathan P. Snow '75				1905–11, 1915–17, 1918–20	
Daniel E. Bradley '85				1906–11, 1914–16	
John L. Mann '98				1906–07	
Arthur W. Hardy '89				1908–09	
Leslie B. Farr '03			1909–10		1909–10
Carroll W. Davis '03					1909–10
Allen Hazen '85	1910–11				1910–11
George F. Hardy '88					1910–11, 1914–15
George C. Stoddard '81	1922–23		1910–22		1910–23
William P. Snow '81				1910–12	
George F. Sparhawk '91				1910–12	
George E. Melendy '85	1911–12				1911–12
William C. Phelps '95		1911–14			1911–14
Wesley G. Carr '84				1911–13	

Name and Class	*President*	*Treasurer*	*Secretary*	*Advisory Board*	*Executive Committee*
Charles A. Holden '01				1911–13, 1919–25	
Arthur C. Tozzer '03	1914–15			1917–19, 1922–26	1912–16
Fred H. Munkelt '09	1929–32		1922–27, 1937–48		1912–13, 1922–32, 1934–48
Maurice F. Brown '98				1912–14	
Frank H. Trow '95				1912–14	
Hardy S. Ferguson '91	1913–14				1913–14
Arthur B. Illsley '95				1913–15, 1917–19	
John P. Brooks D-85				1913–15, 1927–29, 1930–34	
William Hood D-67				1913–15	
Frank E. Cudworth '02		1914–16			1914–18, 1929–32, 1940–46
David H. Andrews D-69				1914–16	
Frank J. Reynolds D-89					1915–17
Charles F. Conn '87				1915–17, 1918–20	
Maurice Readey '11		1916–18			1916–19
Charles F. Chase '89				1916–18, 1927–34	
Frank B. Sanborn '89				1916–18	
Morton O. Withey '05				1916–18, 1920–22, 1929–34	
Thomas T. Whittier '00		1918–21			1918–22
Albert Smith '03				1918–20	
Philip L. Thompson '09		1921–54			1919–54
John G. Andrews '02				1919–21	

Name and Class	*President*	*Treasurer*	*Secretary*	*Advisory Board*	*Executive Committee*
Arthur A. Adams '95				1920–22	
Edward D. Hardy '91				1920–22	
Samuel C. Bartlett '08					1921–22, 1943–46
R. A. Wentworth '79				1921–23	
Harold D. Comstock '04				1921–23	
Charles R. Main '08				1921–23, 1924–34	
Edward A. Wiesman '19				1922–26	
Charles F. Goodrich '06	1923–29				1923–30
Raymond R. Marsden '09				1923–34	
Benjamin Ayer '10				1923–25	
John H. Dunlap '08					1924–27
William J. Montgomery '20			1927–30		1927–30, 1933–34
Rudolph N. Miller '20			1951–54		1926–29, 1951–54
Harold E. Plumer '03				1926–34	
Allen P. Richmond '15	1932–34		1930–32	1926–30	1930–34, 1949–50
Maurice J. Leahy '03					1930–33
Charles F. Jost '27			1932–34		1932–34
				Vice President	
George E. Chamberlin '11					1932–34
John S. Macdonald '14	1934–46			1949–50	1934–46, 1947–50
John W. Guppy '24			1934–37		1934–37
George C. Kisevalter '31					1934–40
William P. Kimball '29					1937–38, 1951–61
Arthur V. Ruggles '03					1937–43
Frederic A. Davidson '15	1946–49				1946–49

Name and Class	*President*	*Treasurer*	*Secretary*	*Vice President*	*Executive Committee*
E. Shaw Cole '31	1953–54		1950–51	1950–51	1946–47, 1950–51, 1953–54
Robert E. Adams '20					1946–47
Richard Hazen D-32					1947–49
Harry A. Ward '10					1948–50
Paul J. Halloran '20	1949–51				1949–51
Frederick A. Davidson, Jr. '41,	1955–56			1954–55	1949–50, 1951–53, 1954–58
Richard H. Ellis '17					1951–54
Paul J. Henegan '49			1957–59		1950–51, 1957–59
Augustine H. Ayres '07	1951–53				1951–53
Nelson L. Doe '13				1952–53	1951–53
Herman O. Dressel '48					1951–55
Herbert F. Darling '27	1954–55			1953–54	1953–55, 1956–59
Charles Y. Hitchcock, Jr. '39	1957–58			1956–57	1953–63
Hugh McLaren, Jr. '40		1954–57			1954–57
Robert T. Barr '42	1960–62		1954–57	1958–60	1954–57, 1958–62, 1963–67
F. Byron Tomlinson '36	1958–60			1957–58	1954–63
Thomas W. Streeter, Jr. '48					1955–58
Victor C. Smith '20				1955–56	1955–56
Howard A. Schroedel '26	1956–57				1956–60
Robert M. Egelhoff '39			1959–62		1956–62
Robert M. McIlwain '51	1962–63	1957–60		1960–62	1957–65
Arthur J. Hendler '49					1957–60

Name and Class	*President*	*Treasurer*	*Secretary*	*Vice President*	*Executive Committee*
Frederick S. Geller '48					1958–61
Gerald D. Sarno '51	1963–65			1962–63	1959–69
Deakers H. Davidson '53		1960–63			1960–63
Paul J. Barnico '51					1960–63
Myron Tribus, U. Cal. '42					1960–69
Byron O. McCoy '34					1961–64
Thomas A. Barr '50			1962–69	1969–	
John M. Devor '41					1962–65
Samuel C. Florman '46	1965–67			1963–65	1963–
Reuben Samuels '47		1963–			1963–
William W. Olmstead '39	1967–69			1965–67	1963–
Stephen M. Olko '47					1964–67
Walter J. Cairns '51	1969–			1967–69	1965–
Warren F. Daniell, Jr. '50			1969–		1966–
Harlan W. Fair '54					1967–
Lawrence H. Schwartz '59					1967–
Thomas L. Jester '64					1969–
David V. Ragone, MIT '51					1969–

APPENDIX D

Dartmouth Society of Engineers Prize Recipients, 1928–1970

June 1928: Timothy Paige, T.S. '29. "*Traffic Congestion and Relief.*"

June 1929: George H. Pasfield, T.S. '29. "*Moffat Tunnel.*"

June 1930: John A. Cooper, D.C. '30. "*Electrification of Steam Railroads.*"

June 1931: Anthony W. VanLeer, T.S. '31. "*Conowingo Hydro-Electric Power Plant.*"

June 1932: George A. Hawkins, T.S. '32. "*Soil Mechanics.*"

June 1933: Chandler B. Griggs, T.S. '33. "*Hydro-Power at Safe Harbor.*"

May 1934: Robert B. Colborn, T.S. '34. "*The Binary Vapor Cycle.*"

May 1935: Gerald M. Hall, T.S. '35. "*History of Civil Engineering.*"

May 1936: George C. Capelle, Jr., D.C. '36. "*Marine Borers.*"

May 1937: Heston S. Hirst, D.C. '36. "*Automatic Sprinklers.*"

May 1938: Henry C. Beck, D.C. '38. "*Labor and the Construction Industry.*"

May 1939: Clement F. Burnap, D.C. '39. "*Labor in Shipyards in the United States.*"

May 1940: G. William Bailey, Jr., T.S. '40. "*The Design of Concrete Forms.*"

May 1941: Willott A. Pitz, T.S. '41. "*Engineering Geology.*"

May 1942: Charles A. Gibbons, Jr., D.C. '42. "*The Plenum Process for Soft Ground and Subaqueous Tunneling.*"

October 1944: David M. Davidson, T.S. '46. "*The Gas Turbine.*"

August 1946: Samuel C. Florman, D.C. '46. "*Lateral Earth Pressure Against Retaining Structures.*"

June 1948: Herman O. Dressel, EE '48. "*The Magnetron Type Vacuum Tube and Its Operation.*"

June 1949: Paul J. Henegan, CE '49. "*Design of Nomographic Charts.*"

June 1950: W. Raymond Evans, Jr., EE '50. "*A Method for Locating an Ellipse in Space.*"

June 1951: Nicholas C. Costes, CE '51. "*A Critical Evaluation of Various Approaches to Column Theory and Design.*"

June 1952: Robert E. Fiertz, ME '52, and John C. Woods, ME '52. "*Determination of Air Velocity by Electric Strain Gage Measurements.*"

June 1953: Merle L. Thorpe, ME '53. "*Lateral Blow-Off of a Bunsen Flame.*"

June 1954: George B. Passano, ME '54. "*Kerosine Mist as a Fuel in a CFR Engine.*"

June 1955: Dana E. Low, CE '55. "*Limit Design of Continuous Beams.*"

June 1956: William L. Pierce, EE '56. "*Compensation of Diehl Ward–Leonard Servo.*"

June 1957: David W. Rice, CE '57. "*Investigation, Design, and Economic Study of a Gravity Dam Consisting of a Reinforced Concrete Shell Filled with Soil.*"

William B. Macurdy, EE '57. "*Analysis and Compensation in Sampled-Data Control Systems.*"

J. William Scher, ME '57. "*Design of Multiple-Ring Dies for Powder Metallurgy.*"

June 1958: William H. Davidow, EE '58. "*The Construction and Testing of a Dynamic Torquemeter.*"

June 1959: Leslie J. Tenn-Lyn, CE '59. "*A Proposed Suspension Stadium Design.*"

June 1960: Neil E. Greene, TT '60. "*An Examination of Hall's Dual Theory of Conductivity in Relation to the Thomson Thermoelectric Effect.*"

Frederick C. Hart, Jr., EE '59. "*An Experimental Study of the Effects of a Resonant Dipole Antenna in a Single Wire Transmission Line Field.*"

June 1961: David Schreur, CE '61. "*Report on Kalamazoo River Pollution.*"

Louis C. Semprebon, MS (EE) '61. "*Measurement of the Direction of Arrival of Atmospheric Whistlers.*"

June 1962: Peter D. Stone, CE '62, and Bruce K. Johnson ME '62. "*Performance Evaluation of the Daedalus Machine.*"

Thomas H. Judd, EE '62. "*Strip-Type Transmission Lines. A Pulse Position Modulated Communication System.*"

June 1963: Stephen P. Lasch, EE '63. "*Effects of Magnetic Activity on Very-Low-Frequency Emissions.*"

June 1964: Richard Van Mell, BE '64. "*A Transportation Study of the Tri-Town Area.*"

June 1965: David W. Heyer, BE '65. "*The Development of a Handwritten Character Input System for Digital Computers.*"

Richard D. Hanson, BME '65. "*The Design of a Box Folding Machine.*"

June 1966: Michael G. Hughes, BE '66. "*The Design and Testing of a Non-Surgical Arterial Bloodflow Probe.*"

June 1967: Benjamin W. Day, BE '67. "*Digital Television Techniques Redundancy Reduction on a Multi-frame Basis.*"

Charles W. Spehrley, Jr., BE '67. "*The Design of a Tape Fed Starting System for Two-Cycle Engines.*"

Paul A. Stokstad, BE '67. "*Design of a Demonstration Electrometer.*"

June 1968: Thomas P. Pearsall, BE '68. "*The Design of Prometheus-I, a General Purpose Output Device for the Interdata-3 Computer.*"

Clay G. Stevens, BE '68. "*Machine Design to Assemble Tungsten Heating Elements.*"

June 1969: Richard Theodore du Moulin, BE '69. "*Water Jet Propulsion for Auxiliary Sailboat Power.*"

June 1970: Anthony S. Donigian, Jr., BE '70. "*A Computer Approach to Water Systems Planning and Evaluation.*"

June 1971: Timothy O. Schad, BE '71. "Sewage Treatment in Rural Areas in Vermont."

APPENDIX E

The Goodrich Prize Recipients 1949–1970

1949: John Hawes McNamara, ME '49
1950: Warren Fisher Daniell, Jr., CE '50
1951: James Phelan Lyons, CE '51
1952: Donald Henry Jorgensen, TT '52
1953: John Craig Hausman, TT '53
1954: John George Avril, TT '54
1955: Dana Evarts Low, CE '55
1956: Thomas Lee Tyler, ME '56
1957: William Bradford Macurdy, EE '57
1958: Martin Carl Anderson, TT '58
1959: Coleman Park Colla, EE '59
1960: James Samuel Picken, EE '60
and
David Adams Spaulding, EE '60
1961: Arthur Feinstein, CE '61
1962: Roger William McArt, ME '62
1963: John F. Walkup, EE '63
1964: Neil Lester Drobny, CE '64
1965: Dale Elwin Runge, ME '65
1966: Edward Anthony Keible, Jr., BE '66
1967: Hector John Motroni, BE '67
1968: John Leonard Brock, BE '68
1969: Douglas Alexander Kerr, BE '69
1970: Thomas Rendal Gilmore, Jr., BE '70
1971: Timothy Owen Schad, BE '71

APPENDIX F

Educational Partners

THE COMPANIES listed below have been Educational Partners of the Thayer School for one year or more since the inception of the Educational Partnership Program in 1966.

The Carpenter Technology Corporation
The Foxboro Company
General Cable Corporation
General Foods Corporation
Hooker Chemical Company
Minnesota Mining and Manufacturing Company
Owens-Illinois, Incorporated
Sanders Associates
Scott Paper Company
The Stanley Works

ENGINEERING ASSOCIATES

In addition to the Educational Partners, the School has been privileged to include the following companies as Engineering Associates. They have generally provided support for special student projects or fellowships:

Anderson-Nichols Company
The Carborundum Company
Chemical Bank New York Trust Company
Continental Oil Company
Digital Systems Corporation
E. I. Du Pont de Nemours & Company
Ford Motor Company
General Electric Company
General Telephone and Electronics Laboratories
Gillette Safety Razor Company
Hercules Incorporated
Honeywell Incorporated
S. C. Johnson and Sons, Incorporated
Jones & Laughlin Steel Corporation
Joy Manufacturing Company

Levitt and Sons, Incorporated
Mobil Research and Development Corporation
New England Power Service Company
Charles Pfizer and Company, Incorporated
Polaroid Corporation
Rockwell Manufacturing
Stauffer Chemical Company
Time Share Corporation
Toro Manufacturing Company

Subject Index

Index of Names